HEALING - THE SHAMAN'S WAY
BOOK 8
TRANSFORMATIVE OILS

Norman W. Wilson PhD

**HEALING - THE SHAMAN'S WAY
BOOK 8
TRANSFORMATIVE OILS**

Cover Design by
S.R. Walker Designs
www.srwalkerdesigns.com

Interior Design
Omar Lopez, PhD

FICTION4ALL

A FICTION4ALL PAPERBACK

©Copyright 2025

Norman W. Wilson, PhD
The right of Norman W. Wilson to be identified as author and channel of this work has been asserted by him in accordance with the Copyright, Designs and Patents Act 1988.

All Rights Reserved

No reproduction, copy or transmission of the publication may be made without written permission.

No paragraph of this publication may be reproduced, copied, or transmitted say with the written permission of the publisher, or in accordance with the provisions of the Copyright Act 1956 (as amended).

Any person who does any unauthorized act in relation to his publication may be liable to criminal prosecution and civil claims for damages.

ISBN: 978 1 78695 914 0

Published by Fiction4All.
www.fiction4all.com
This edition published 2025

DISCLAIMER

The author offers no guarantees that any of the procedures or suggestions described herein will work. Before following any of the suggestions, always consult your medical practitioner. Persons under eighteen should not attempt any of the suggested activities. You are responsible for how you use the information contained in this book.

EDITORIAL NOTE

This book is more than a revision and update of book 7. New content and recipes have significantly changed the focus.

Norman W. Wilson, PhD

ALSO, BY NORMAN W. WILSON

Books
Shamanism: What It's All About
So, You Think You Want To Be A Buddhist?
Promethean Necessity And Its Implications for Humanity
DUH! The American Educational Disaster
The Sayings of Esaugetuh: The Master of Breath
A Shaman's Journey Revealed Through Poetry with Gavriel Navarro
The Shaman's Quest
The Shaman's Transformation
The Shaman's War
The Shaman's Genesis
The Shaman's Revelations
The Making of A Shaman
Activating Your Spirit Guides
Healing-The Shaman's Way
How To Make Moral and Ethical Decisions: A Guide
Teas, Soups, and Salads
Reiki: The Instructor's Manual
Shamanic Healing: Book One
Shamanic Healing Book Two: Crystals
Healing-The Shaman's Way: Herbs That Help You Heal: Book Three
Healing-The Shaman's Way: Using Essential Oils: Book Four
Healing-The Shaman's Way: Vibrations To Heal Book Five
Healing-The Shaman's Way: Shamanism and Spirituality Book Six

Courses
At Udemy.com
Healing-The Shaman's Way
Healing-The Shaman's Way Using Crystals
Healing-The Shaman's Way Using Herbs

Healing-The Shaman's Way Using Essential Oils
Healing-The Shaman's Way Using Vibration to Heal
Healing-The Shaman's Way Religion VS Spirituality

<u>Lectures*</u>
On YouTube.com
Protecting Yourself
How To Get What You Really Want
The Seven Attributes of Selfhood
Mirror, Mirror
*There are 20 additional lectures available on YouTube.

CHAPTER ONE

Welcome to the World of Transformative Essential Oils!

Essential oils have been a cornerstone of natural wellness for thousands of years. Evidence from Ancient Egypt points to their use as far back as 4500 BCE, and China's *Yellow Emperor's Book of Internal Medicine* (2697–2597 BCE) also details their medicinal properties. This ancient wisdom inspires modern practices, providing a powerful connection with nature's healing potential.

So, what exactly are essential oils? The term "essential" refers to the crucial components of a plant needed for its survival—those elements that give the plant its distinctive aroma and therapeutic qualities. These oils are not just fragrant; they are concentrated extracts from plant cells that contain powerful chemical compounds known to have medicinal benefits.

A Vast World of Healing Plants

An estimated 320,000 plant species exist worldwide, and about 80,000 have known medicinal value. That number continues to grow as scientists discover new properties through research.

However, with the increasing availability of essential oils in stores, small shops, and online marketplaces, it's important to make sure you're getting high-quality oils. Not all essential oils are created equal, and the purity and potency of the oils you purchase can vary significantly. Here are a few tips to ensure you are selecting the best:

How to Choose Quality Essential Oils:

1. Look for both the **common and scientific names** of the plant on the label.
2. Check that the **method of production** is clearly identified.
3. Ensure the bottle is made of **dark glass** (blue, green, or amber) to protect the oil from light degradation.
4. Confirm the **part(s) of the plant** used to create the oil.
5. Check for **certifications** like USDA Organic, PETA Cruelty-Free, Leaping Bunny, and non-GMO statements.

The Science Behind Essential Oils

Essential oils are typically divided into two main categories based on their chemical constituents: **Hydrocarbons** and **Oxygenated Compounds**.

- **Hydrocarbons**, including **terpenes**, are known to support detoxification by helping the liver and kidneys clear toxins.
- **Oxygenated Compounds**, such as **Esters**, are the result of reactions between alcohols and acids. These compounds are prized for their antifungal properties and ability to promote relaxation and calm.

The scent of an essential oil is more than just pleasant—it has the potential to influence our emotions, memories, and even physical healing. Here are five ways essential oils may impact you:

1. **Enhance inner peace** and boost self-esteem.
2. Help you see both the **good and bad** in situations, fostering personal growth.
3. Affect your **emotional state** by influencing your temperament and mood.
4. **Accelerate healing** by stimulating the body's natural repair processes.
5. Promote **relaxation**, aiding in the overall healing process.

Essential Oils and Their Risks

While essential oils offer a wealth of benefits, they must be used with care. Some oils—especially those with strong fragrances—contain compounds like **limonene**, **citronellol**, **eugenol**, and **linalool**, which may irritate sensitive individuals.

A general rule of thumb is never to apply essential oils undiluted directly to your skin. The exception is **Frankincense**, which can be safely applied around the outer edges of a non-healing wound to aid in infection control and encourage natural healing.

Before using any essential oil, it's recommended to do a **patch test**: apply a small amount of oil to a discreet area of the skin. If you notice redness, swelling, or itching, discontinue use immediately and wash the area with mild soap and warm water. Always consult your healthcare provider if any irritation persists.

Similarly, when using oils in diffusers, sprays, or incense, it's wise to perform a **sniff test**. If you experience any irritation to your eyes, nose, or throat, stop using the product.

What Are Essential Oils?

Essential oils are concentrated, hydrophobic (water-repelling) liquids derived from plants. They are often called **volatile oils** due to their ability to evaporate quickly into the air, releasing their distinctive aroma. True essential oils are always plant-based and are not created synthetically. They are extracted from specialized plant cells that house the precious compounds that give each oil its unique properties.

How Are Essential Oils Made?

There are several methods used to extract oils from plants, and choosing the right method depends on the type of oil and its intended use. Here are the nine main methods:

1. Steam Distillation
2. Absolute Extraction
3. Cold Press
4. CO_2 Extraction
5. Mechanical Expression
6. Water Distillation
7. Solvent Extraction
8. Enfleurage
9. Maceration

Four Essential Oil Extraction Methods: An In-Depth Look

This section will focus on four common extraction methods used to create essential oils: **Steam Distillation, CO2 Extraction, Maceration,** and **Water Distillation**. Each method has its unique advantages and challenges, and understanding them will help you appreciate the complexities of essential oil production.

Steam Distillation: The Traditional Method

Steam distillation is by far the most widely used method for extracting essential oils. This method involves the use of a specialized apparatus known as a **still**, typically made of stainless steel. The process unfolds in several steps:

1. **The Still**: Plant material is placed into a container within the still. Steam is introduced into the plant material, and the heat causes the essential oils to vaporize.
2. **Condensation**: The vapor travels through a cooling system (a condenser), where it condenses back into liquid form.
3. **Separation**: Because essential oils do not mix with water, they float to the top of the liquid mixture, where they can be siphoned off.

For personal use, consider a small still. They can be purchased online for around $80. Larger, more professional stills can cost upwards of $1,300.

One important aspect of steam distillation is the **density** of the essential oil. Some oils, such as **clove, cinnamon**, and **vetiver**, are denser than water and will sink to the bottom during distillation.

The steam distillation process has its challenges. The heat required for distillation can damage the delicate compounds in the oil, altering its quality and reducing its effectiveness. This is where other extraction methods, such as **CO2 Extraction**, can provide a solution.

CO2 Extraction: A Higher-Quality Oil

Though steam distillation is the most common method, **CO2 Extraction** is often considered the superior technique for producing high-quality essential oils. The main advantage of CO2 extraction is its ability to extract oils without the need for high heat. Here's how it works:

1. **Pressurization**: Carbon dioxide (CO2) is pressurized until it becomes a liquid.
2. **Solvent Action**: This liquid CO2 is pumped into a container filled with plant material, where it acts as a solvent, dissolving the essential oils.
3. **Separation**: The CO2 is then returned to its natural pressure, evaporates, and leaves behind the pure essential oil.

One of the major benefits of the CO2 extraction process is that it does not use harmful solvents, making it both safer for humans and more environmentally friendly. The resulting oil is typically thicker and more concentrated, with a more pronounced aroma.

Maceration: The Art of Infused Oils

While steam distillation and CO2 extraction are widely used for essential oils, **Maceration** is a gentler, simpler method typically used for creating **infused oils**. This process is most commonly used to extract the essence of flowers, and it involves soaking plant material in warm carrier oils. Here's how it works:

1. **Preparation**: Dry plant materials (such as flowers) are ground into a coarse powder. Moisture in the plant material can lead to rancidity, so it's important to ensure the plant is dry. Some oils, like **Vitamin E** or **Wheatgerm Oil**, are added to prevent rancidity.
2. **Soaking**: The plant material is placed in a sealed container, and a solvent (typically a carrier oil) is added.
3. **Shaking**: The mixture is shaken occasionally for up to a week.
4. **Straining and Pressing**: After a week, the liquid is strained. The remaining plant material is then pressed to extract any remaining oil.
5. **Clarification**: The liquid is filtered to remove impurities, and it may change color as a result of the infusion process.
6. **Storage**: The infused oil is placed in a dark glass container and stored in a cool, dry place for up to 12 months.

This method is ideal for capturing the heavier, larger molecules of plants, which may not be as easily extracted through distillation. While macerated oils may not be as concentrated as steam-distilled oils, they still offer a unique, richly infused product.

Water Distillation: A DIY-Friendly Option

For those looking for a more affordable, at-home option, **Water Distillation** provides a practical and accessible method for essential oil extraction. Unlike the more industrial methods of steam and CO2 distillation, water distillation is simpler and more budget-friendly, making it a great option for DIY enthusiasts.

Carrier Oils and Their Uses

In the world of essential oils, **carrier oils** play an essential role. But what exactly are carrier oils, and why are they so important when using essential oils? Can adding a carrier oil to an essential oil compromise its purity?

What are Carrier Oils?

A **carrier oil**—sometimes referred to as a **base oil**—is a mild oil used to dilute potent essential oils before application to the skin. The purpose of carrier oils is to **carry** the essential oil onto the skin and protect it from potential irritation. Some essential oils are highly concentrated and can be too intense or even harmful if applied directly to the skin without dilution.

For example, **oregano oil** is a powerful essential oil that can cause skin burns if not properly diluted. This is why it is strongly recommended to always use a carrier oil when applying essential oils, especially for individuals with sensitive skin. Additionally, before using any essential oil, it's essential to perform a **patch test**. Simply apply a small amount of diluted oil to a discreet area of the skin and wait for any adverse reaction (like redness or swelling). If irritation occurs, discontinue use immediately and consult your healthcare provider.

Carrier oils are also used in certain applications, such as the **layering method**, which will be discussed in detail later in the course.

Recommended Carrier Oils: Here's a list of some commonly used carrier oils, each with its unique properties and benefits. These oils are commonly used to dilute essential oils without compromising their effectiveness while offering their beneficial properties for the skin.

- **Borage Oil**
- **Jojoba Oil**
- **Walnut Oil**
- **Macadamia Oil**
- **Sweet Almond Oil**
- **Rosehip Oil**
- **Argan Oil**
- **Fractionated Coconut Oil**
- **Grapeseed Oil**
- **Avocado Oil**
- **Neem Oil**
- **Castor Oil**
- **Hemp Seed Oil**
- **Olive Oil**
- **Vitamin E Oil**
- **Wheatgerm Oil**

Avoiding Issues with Essential Oils

While essential oils offer a wide range of benefits, it's important to be mindful of potential sensitivities or allergies. Some people may experience irritation due to

certain components found in essential oils, particularly those with a strong fragrance. Additionally, incorrect or overuse can create problems. Following is a list of the common irritants, the essential oils in which they are found, and suggested safe handling.

Limonene is found in Citrus Oils such as lemons, oranges, grapefruits, and bergamots. It is a skin irritant. Always dilute before applying to your skin.

Citronellol is found in geranium, rose, and citronella. It is a potential skin allergen. Do a patch test before use, and use a low concentration in blends.

Eugenol is found in clove, cinnamon, and bay leaf. It is a skin irritant and may cause mucous membrane issues. Avoid using it if you have sensitive skin. Be sure to use surgical gloves when handling high concentrations.

Linalool occurs in lavender, coriander, and basil. It is a skin irritant. It should be stored in airtight containers and replaced every couple of years.

The bottom line is to always use caution and check with your medical practitioner if you have questions or experience issues. The primary function and use of Essential Oils is to help ease, reduce, or eliminate a problem; not to create one.

CHAPTER TWO

Folded Essential Oils

Folded Essential Oils are oils that have undergone a special process to enhance their potency and fragrance. The process involves multiple distillations or fractionations. Sometimes the oils are blended with other compounds to intensify their aroma or therapeutic potential. Folded Essential Oils are used in perfumery and sometimes in skincare products. If you choose to use Folded Essential Oils, be sure you use only a drop or two with a carrier oil. They are powerful. With that said, here are seven potential downsides to using Folded Oils.

Environmentally, there are concerns about the necessary additional resources and energy required to make Folded Essential Oils.

If the folded essential oils are applied directly, your skin may experience strong sensitization or irritation, and serious allergic reactions may occur.

Folded essential oils can interact negatively with medications. If you have medical issues, always consult your dermatologist or primary physician before using Them.

The scent may be overpowering and cause headaches or dizziness.

Increased Toxicity may occur with higher concentrations, particularly if the oils are incorrectly used.

Potential Overuse can occur because of a tendency to use Folded Essential Oils more often when the aroma of the oils fades is a factor because Folded Essential Oils tend to be more expensive than regular essential oils.

In fairness, Folded Essential Oils can be effective in addressing certain issues that require more intense treatment. Here are seven issues that may benefit from using Folded Essential Oils.

Severe Anxiety may be relieved by using Folded Essential Oils in a diffuser.

Pain management of muscle soreness, joint pain, and headaches is improved with Folded Essential Oils such as peppermint or eucalyptus. Used in a diffuser or applied directly to the skin. (Must be mixed with a carrier oil.)

Sleep disorders may be reduced by using Folded Lavender or Chamomile Essential Oils.

Respiratory Issues may be lessened by using Folded Eucalyptus or Peppermint Essential Oils.

Skin problems may be helped with Tea Tree or Frankincense Folded Essential Oils.

Mood Swings may benefit from the enhanced potency of Folded Bergamot or Lemon Essential Oils.

Detoxification of the body may be enhanced using Folded Juniper Essential Oil.

As you continue your journey into the world of essential oils, it's important to keep a few key points in mind:

- **Subjectivity of Use**: Many claims about the benefits of essential oils are anecdotal and subjective.
- **Lack of Scientific Evidence**: While some studies show the effectiveness of essential oils, conclusive scientific proof may not always be readily available.
- **Not the Only Oils for the Job**: The oils discussed here may not be the only ones that can serve the purposes outlined. Depending on your needs, there are many alternatives for you to consider.

RECIPES

Here are four recipes for Folded Essential Oil Blends: Anxiety, Pain relief, Skin conditions, Mood swings.

What You Will Need:

In addition to the Folded Essential Oils mentioned in each of the four recipes, you will need a 10 ml roller bottle, a 10 ml glass bottle, a 20 ml dropper bottle with a dropper, and a small diffuser. (To do these recipes at home)

Anxiety Relief

Ingredients:
5 drops of Lavender Essential Oil
3 drops of Bergamot Essential Oil
2 drops of Frankincense Essential Oil
10 ml of carrier oil (Jojoba or Sweet Almond)

Instructions:
1. Combine all the ingredients in a 10 ml roller bottle.
2. Shake the bottle for about 30 seconds.
3. Gently apply to each side of the back of your neck and **one swipe across your forehead.** Do this at bedtime and when you get up in the morning.

You may also opt to apply this during the day. If you do, roll it on each **wrist, and gently rub them together for 20 seconds.**

Pain Relief

Ingredients:
4 drops of Peppermint Folded Essential Oil
4 drops of Eucalyptus Folded Essential Oil
2 drops of Clove Folded Essential Oil
10 ml of carrier oils (Consider Fractionated Coconut Oil)

Instructions:
Mix all ingredients in a small, clean glass bottle.
Warm the bottled oils (Under the hot water faucet).
     Massage a small amount into the affected area.
Avoid broken skin or sensitive areas.

Skin Conditions (Acne, Eczema, etc.)

Ingredients:
3 drops of Tea Tree Folded Essential Oil

3 drops of Chamomile Folded Essential Oil
3 drops of Geranium Folded Essential Oil
10 ml of carrier oil (Argan or Rosehip oil)
Instructions:
Blend oils in a dropper bottle.
Apply a small amount to the affected area twice a day.

Mood Swings:

Ingredients:
4 drops of Sweet Orange Folded Essential Oil
3 drops of Ylang-Ylang Folded Essential Oil
2 drops of Sandalwood Folded Essential Oil
15 ml of carrier oil (Grapeseed Oil)
Instructions:
Add 2 to 3 drops of the mixed oils to a diffuser or place the mixture in a roller bottle.
Use as a personal scent or in the diffuser for 20 to 30 minutes.

CHAPTER THREE

Six Basic Essential Oils

This chapter focuses on six regular essential oils and their potential transformative benefits: red Mandarin, Silver Fir, Helichrysum, Ho Wood, Holy Basil, and Black Spruce.

Red Mandarin Essential Oil

Red Mandarin oil is a **cold-pressed** essential oil made from the outer peel of the mandarin fruit. This oil has a sweet, yet tart aroma. It is commonly used to brighten the atmosphere when it is added to a diffuser. In the U.S., Red Mandarin Oil is often referred to as Tangerine oil.

Benefits of Red Mandarin

Fatigue or Low Mood: If you're feeling tired or down, blend 2 eyedroppers of Red Mandarin with 4 eyedroppers of a carrier oil like Jojoba. Put the mixture in a roll-on bottle, shake it well, and apply to your wrists. Rub your wrists together for a couple of seconds, and you'll begin to feel a lift in your mood.

Abdominal Bloating: You can also apply the same blend around your abdomen to help relieve bloating.

Circulation Boost: To improve circulation, use the roll-on blend on your wrists before bed and in the morning.

Red Mandarin works especially well when paired with essential oils like Holy Basil, Bergamot, Spikenard, or Rosemary.

Silver Fir Essential Oil

Silver Fir essential oil is steam-distilled and offers a refreshing, woodsy aroma. However, it's important to consult with your healthcare provider before using this oil if you have any of the following conditions: Cancer, Epilepsy, Liver issues, Pregnancy, and Children under 2 years old.

Benefits of Silver Fir:

Respiratory Support: Silver Fir is great for addressing respiratory issues such as bronchitis, colds, or flu symptoms. Add 5 drops to a diffuser to help clear your sinuses and alleviate fatigue.

Muscle Pain: To relieve muscular discomfort, blend 4 drops of Silver Fir with **6** eyedroppers of a carrier oil, like Jojoba. Apply to sore areas.

Seasonal Affective Disorder: Combine 3 drops of Silver Fir with Orange essential oil in a diffuser to support a positive mood during the darker months. Small personal diffusers are perfect for use in a home office or on a nightstand in your bedroom.

Helichrysum Essential Oil

Helichrysum, part of the Sunflower family, is an oil derived from all parts of the plant, including its dried leaves. The oil has a unique aroma, often described as light curry.

Benefits of Helichrysum:

Healing and Inflammation: Known for its anti-inflammatory, antifungal, and antibacterial properties, Helichrysum promotes healing and reduces inflammation. It can be used for a variety of issues, including:

Skin irritations, bloating, indigestion, and acid reflux.

Allergy and Cold Relief: Helichrysum is also helpful for reducing allergy symptoms and soothing coughs associated with colds.

How to Use: For skin irritation, dilute 2-3 drops of Helichrysum in 1 tablespoon of Jojoba oil. Apply a small amount to the affected area once or twice daily for up to three days. If irritation persists, consult a dermatologist.

For a cough, boil two cups of water and pour it into a bowl. Add 1-2 drops of Helichrysum Essential Oil. Drape a towel over your head, lean over the bowl, and inhale deeply for 5 to 10 minutes.

For relief of nighttime coughing, add 3 to 6 drops of Helichrysum Essential Oil to a diffuser and turn it on for 30 minutes to one hour.

Ho Wood Essential Oil

Ho Wood is derived from the camphor tree, and its oil is produced through steam distillation. The bark and wood of the tree are used in the extraction process. Ho Wood has a sweet, woodsy scent. People find Ho Wood to be calming.

Benefits of Ho Wood:

Cold and Flu Relief: Ho Wood can help alleviate symptoms of colds and flu, as well as muscular pain and wounds.

Mental Clarity: It's also known for helping reduce stress and mental instability, improving focus and overall emotional well-being.

Immune Support: Ho Wood boosts the immune system, eases headaches, and helps combat parasites and skin infections.

Ho Wood blends beautifully with essential oils such as Clary Sage, Frankincense, and Lavender for a more personalized aroma and therapeutic effect.

Ho Wood Recipe: Inducing Transformative Peaceful Thoughts for Positive Dreams

What you will need:

Ho Wood Essential Oil
Bergamot Essential Oil
Juniper Essential Oil
Mandarin Essential Oil
One essential oil inhaler (available online for $7–$20)
A pair of sterilized tweezers

A ¼ oz measuring cup

Optional: If you don't have an inhaler, use a cotton ball, a small bottle, or a small dish.

Directions:

Start by placing 6 drops of Jojoba carrier oil into a sterilized dish.

Add 3 drops each of Ho Wood, Bergamot, Juniper, and Mandarin Essential Oils to the dish. Mix thoroughly.

Using sterilized tweezers, place the cotton wick insert from the inhaler into the mixture, ensuring it's fully saturated.

Return the wick to the inhaler and securely close the parts.

To use, close one nostril and hold the inhaler near the other. Breathe in deeply, then switch nostrils and repeat. Use this inhaler twice a day, ideally before bedtime.

Shake the inhaler a couple of times before each use to refresh the blend.

Alternative Method: If you don't have an inhaler, you can place the oil blend in a small dish, hold it up to your nose, and inhale deeply.

Holy Basil (Tulsi) Essential Oil

It's important not to confuse Holy Basil with the common culinary basil. Holy Basil, called **Tulsi**, is highly revered for its medicinal benefits. All parts of the plant are used, each addressing different health concerns.

Health Benefits of Holy Basil:

Reduces stress, improves sleep, enhances memory and focus, aids in repairing ulcers, lowers blood sugar and cholesterol, releases intestinal gas, and soothes sore muscles.

Caution: Avoid Holy Basil if you are pregnant, breastfeeding, undergoing cancer treatment, or dealing with serious heart or skin conditions. Always consult your doctor before using essential oils.

Patch Test for Holy Basil:

Before using Holy Basil, perform a patch test to ensure your skin doesn't react.

Mix 1 drop of Holy Basil with 4 drops of carrier oil in a small dish.

Apply a small amount of the mixture to your wrist using your finger.

Wait **for 30 minutes** to check for redness or irritation. If any reaction occurs, wash the area thoroughly and consult your doctor before proceeding with further use.

Holy Basil Recipe for Soothing Sore Muscles

If you experience sore muscles, this blend can help provide relief:

Ingredients:

2–3 drops of Holy Basil Essential Oil
Your favorite carrier oil

Directions:

Mix the Holy Basil oil with your carrier oil.
Gently massage the mixture into the affected area.

Add this blend to your bath with 2 tablespoons of Epsom salt for an extra boost for relaxation and muscle relief.

Black Spruce Essential Oil

Black Spruce is derived from the Picea Mariana tree, with its needles and branches being distilled to create this grounding and calming oil. Its **woodsy aroma** helps restore balance and is ideal for promoting relaxation.

Benefits of Black Spruce:

- Supports skin health
- Enhances calmness and emotional balance
- Alleviates respiratory issues
- Boosts the immune system
- Eases arthritis and gout pain
- Improves sleep
- Supports hair health

Recipe for Sleep Improvement with Black Spruce

Ingredients:

- 5 drops of Black Spruce Essential Oil
- 5 drops of Cedarwood Essential Oil
- 5 drops of Frankincense Essential Oil
- Water (for your diffuser)

1. Add 5 drops each of Black Spruce, Cedarwood, and Frankincense oils into your diffuser.
2. Fill the diffuser with water as directed by its instructions.
3. Place the diffuser in your bedroom and turn it on about 20 minutes before bedtime. Let it run until it automatically shuts off.
4. Enjoy a restful night's sleep enhanced by the calming properties of these essential oils.

Recipe for Beard and Mustache Care

For men struggling with coarse facial hair or skin issues beneath the beard, this blend can help soften the hair and soothe the skin underneath. It also promotes hair growth and reduces dandruff.

Ingredients:

- 6 drops of Frankincense Essential Oil
- 8 drops of Black Spruce Essential Oil
- 5 drops of Cedarwood Essential Oil
- 5 drops of Bergamot Essential Oil
- 30 drops of Jojoba Oil

Directions:

1. Combine all the oils in a dark-colored bottle with a dropper.
2. Apply 2 to 3 drops after a morning shower for a soft beard and improved skin health.

Final Reminder:

To preserve the integrity and potency of your essential oils, store them in a dark, cool, and dry place. Exposure to light can degrade the oils and reduce their effectiveness. It is always a good idea to use dark-colored glass bottles for storage.

CHAPTER FOUR

Working with Transformative Essential Oils

Cold Pressing

Homemade Transformative Orange Essential Oil For Pain

Cold pressing is an easy and cost-effective method for creating essential oils that can be done at home. Because you are investing your time, you are building ownership in your physical transformation. To continue that transformation, here is a simple guide for making a massage oil to relieve pain and to make your day a bit better.

RECIPE

What You Will Need:

- 25 to 35 large ripe oranges
- 1 paring knife
- 1 thermometer
- 1 pot for boiling water
- 1 juicer
- 1/4 measuring cup
- 1 small sterilized bottle with a stopper
- 1 juice pitcher
- 1 garlic press
- 4 to 6 ounces of Jojoba oil (or another carrier oil)

Directions:

1. **Prepare the Oranges**: Remove any stickers from the oranges. Then clean the oranges with a cloth soaked in lavender hydrosol. If you don't have hydrosol, tap water will work fine... Rinse and dry the oranges
2. **Peel the Oranges**: Carefully peel each orange, setting the peel aside. Be sure to remove the white pith, as it can absorb juice.
3. **Cut the Peels**: Cut the orange peels into 1-inch pieces.
4. **Heat the Peels**: Place the cut peels into a pot and add enough water to cover them. Heat the water to **120°F** (use your thermometer to check). Once it reaches the desired temperature, remove it from the heat and let it sit for 10 minutes.
5. **Press the Peels**: Use a garlic press to extract the oil from the orange peels. Place the pressed oil into the measuring cup. Continue pressing until all the peel is used.
6. **Mix the Oils**: Combine the extracted orange oil with 4 to 6 ounces of Jojoba oil (or your preferred carrier oil) in a sterilized bottle.
7. **Juice the Oranges**: Juice the oranges and refrigerate the juice for later use.
8. **Dispose of the Pulp**: Discard the leftover pulp.

Before using the Orange Essential Oil for a massage, warm the bottle in your hands for a minute, shake it well to mix the oils, and then have your partner apply a few drops to your back.

Petitgrain Essential Oil To Calm and Uplift

Petitgrain Essential Oil is made from the **twigs, leaves, and branches** of the Bitter Orange Tree. It has a fresh, citrusy scent and blends well with other citrus and wood oils.

Petitgrain offers a variety of benefits:

Benefits:

- Uplifts the spirit
- Calms and balances emotions
- Eases anxiety
- Reduces insomnia and stress
- Clears up acne and oily skin

How to Use Petitgrain Essential Oil:

1. **Stress Relief**: For quick anxiety relief, rub a small amount of Petitgrain oil on one wrist, then rub both wrists together for a few seconds.
2. **Insomnia**: Add 4 drops of Petitgrain Essential Oil to your diffuser, following the manufacturer's instructions. Please turn it on before going to bed to promote restful sleep.
3. **Acne or Oily Skin**: Combine 2 drops of Petitgrain Essential Oil with 3 drops of Jojoba oil. Apply the mixture to acne-prone or oily skin areas. After 15–20 minutes, wash your face with a mild soap.

Sunpati Essential Oil To Relax and Induce Sleep

Sunpati Essential Oil, with the botanical name **Rhododendron**, has long been used for medicinal purposes, including as an herbal tea. The oil is distilled from the flowers of the plant and offers the following benefits:

Benefits of Sunpati Essential Oil:

- Supports the respiratory system
- Acts as a decongestant
- Relieves sore joints and aching muscles
- Eases tension and induces relaxation
- Grounds for meditation
- Promotes restful sleep
- Strengthens feelings of security and empowerment

Sunpati Essential Oil is particularly useful for those seeking emotional balance and relaxation, especially during stressful times or when preparing for meditation.

What You Will Need:

- One quality diffuser with a timer
- 1/4 to 1/2 cup of distilled water (tap water will also work)
- 4 to 8 drops of Sunpati Essential Oil

Note: Sunpati Essential Oil blends well with Clary Sage, Rose, Pine, Lemon, and Lavender. If desired, reduce the amount of

Sunpati by two drops and add one of these complementary oils.

Directions:

1. Place the diffuser in your bedroom.
2. Add the distilled water and essential oil(s) to the diffuser.
3. Turn it on 15 to 30 minutes before bedtime.

Sunpati Recipe to Relieve Pain in Muscles

Muscle pain is a widespread issue, affecting an estimated 1.7 billion people worldwide. Lower back pain alone is the leading cause of disability in 160 countries. Essential oils, which are both cost-effective and natural, have become a popular remedy. Sunpati Essential Oil is particularly effective in relieving muscle pain.

What You Will Need:

- 4 to 5 drops of Sunpati Essential Oil
- 2 drops of Clary Sage Essential Oil
- 8 drops of a carrier oil (e.g., Jojoba Oil)
- 1 small mixing bowl

Directions:

1. Thoroughly mix all the oils in the bowl.
2. For enhanced effectiveness, gently warm the mixture, ensuring it does not overheat.
3. Massage the warm oil blend into the affected muscles or lower back.

ROSE ESSENTIAL OIL

Rose Essential Oil is among the most expensive essential oils, and with good reason. It takes approximately 252,000 rose petals (80,000 roses) to produce just 5ml of oil. Pure rose essential oil—the only kind recommended for use—is extremely potent. Due to its high concentration, Rose Essential Oil should never be applied directly to the skin; always dilute it with a carrier oil.

Key Transformative Properties: Rose Essential Oil is renowned for its antidepressant, antiseptic, antispasmodic, hemostatic, and neuroprotective qualities. Below is an overview of its potential benefits:

Skin Benefits:

- Helps clear up acne
- Improves scar appearance
- Soothes skin irritations
- Reduces pore size

Emotional and Physical Benefits:

- Alleviates anxiety, depression, and stress
- Reduces headache pain
- Relieves menstrual cramps

A caution:

- Side effects may include nausea, vomiting, diarrhea, or eye redness.
- Rose Essential Oil is not safe for use during pregnancy, as it may lead to miscarriage or abnormal bleeding.

Bath or Foot Soak for Stress Relief: Rose Essential Oil can provide much-needed relief from stress and pain through a relaxing bath or foot soak.

Recipe for Rose Essential Oil Bath:

What You Will Need:

- 10 drops of Rose Essential Oil
- 1 ounce of carrier oil
- A Turkish bath towel or terry cloth robe

Directions:

1. Mix the essential oil with the carrier oil.
2. Draw a hot bath and test the water temperature for comfort.
3. Add the oil mixture to the bathwater.
4. Soak for 15 to 20 minutes.
5. After the bath, wrap yourself in the towel or robe and relax for 10 to 20 minutes.

Recipe for Rose Essential Oil Foot Bath:

What You Will Need:

- A pan large enough to accommodate your feet

- Warm water (enough to cover your feet)
- A soft towel
- 10 drops of Rose Essential Oil
- 15 to 20 drops of carrier oil
- A chair or stool

Directions:

1. Heat the water to a comfortable temperature.
2. Mix the Rose Essential Oil with the carrier oil.
3. Add the oil mixture to the warm water and stir well.
4. Test the water temperature with one foot. If comfortable, soak both feet for 10 to 15 minutes.
5. Consider including 5 drops of Rosemary Essential Oil for an added boost.

Transformative Rose Essential Oil to Reduce Anxiety, Stress, And Depression

1. **Massage:**

Mix 4 drops of Rose Essential Oil, 2 drops of Frankincense Essential Oil, and 10 drops of carrier oil. Massage gently into the skin.

2. **Inhaler:**

Add 5 drops of Rose Essential Oil to an inhaler. If unavailable, place the oil on a small plate and inhale deeply through one nostril at a time. Repeat twice, wait 10 minutes, and repeat if necessary.

3. **Diffuser:**

Add Rose Essential Oil to a diffuser, following the manufacturer's instructions.

Recipe for Rose Essential Oil Foot Bath

What You Will Need:

- A pan big enough to hold water and your feet
- Warm water to cover your feet
- A soft towel
- 10 drops of Rose Essential Oil
- 15–20 drops of carrier oil
- A chair or stool

Directions:

1. Heat the water until warm but not too hot.
2. Mix the Rose Essential Oil with the carrier oil.
3. Add the oil mixture to the warm water and stir thoroughly.
4. Test the water temperature with one foot. If comfortable, immerse both feet and soak for 10–15 minutes.
5. Optional: To enhance the experience, add 5 drops of Rosemary Essential Oil.

Benefits of Rose Essential Oil

In today's world, physical and emotional stress, anxiety, and depression are common challenges. Instead of relying on medications, consider the use of essential oils to alleviate these issues. Rose Essential Oil can help relieve anxiety, stress, and depression in three main ways:

1. **Massage**

Mix 4 drops of Rose Essential Oil and 2 drops of Frankincense Essential Oil with 10 drops of carrier oil.

Use the mixture to massage your body or target specific areas like the neck, shoulders, or hands.

2. **Inhaler**

    Add 5 drops of Rose Essential Oil to a personal inhaler. If you don't have one, place the oil on a small plate.

Inhale through one nostril at a time, repeating the process twice. Wait 10 minutes, then repeat.

3. **Diffuser**

Add Rose Essential Oil to a diffuser according to the manufacturer's instructions to create a calming atmosphere.

Creating Your Own Rose Essential Oil

What You Will Need:

- A large glass jar with a lid
- Fresh, pesticide-free rose petals
- Carrier oil (e.g., almond oil, jojoba oil, or olive oil)
- Cheesecloth or a fine strainer
- A dark-colored bottle with a rubber stopper

Directions:

1. Collect fresh roses from a fragrant bush early in the morning. Separate the petals, ensuring they are pesticide-free.
2. Lay the petals on a screen or paper towels, weighted at the edges, to dry in the sun. This step prevents mold formation.
3. Fill a glass jar ¾ full with the dried petals, gently packing them down.
4. Pour carrier oil into the jar until it is full. Secure the lid tightly and shake vigorously.
5. Place the jar in a sunny spot for 2–3 weeks. Bring it inside at night and shake daily.
6. After 2–3 weeks, strain the oil through cheesecloth or a fine strainer to remove the petals. Discard the petals.
7. Transfer the oil to a dark-colored bottle with a rubber stopper for storage.

Usage:
Apply the patch test before applying it to your skin. If you have no negative side effects, you can apply your homemade

Rose Essential Oil diluted with a carrier oil to your face, hands, and feet, or use it in massages.

CHAPTER FIVE
Working with Essential Oils: Continued

Straits Research estimated the market size for essential oils in 2024 to be 24.75 billion dollars. While the popularity of essential oils as alternative medicine is staggering, the rapid growth raises concerns. Essential oils should never replace sound medical treatment. Many claims surrounding their efficacy lack substantial research and may simply result from a placebo effect. However, as I often say, if you feel it works and you feel better. does it matter if it's a placebo? Hardly!

Blending Essential Oils

Blending involves combining compatible essential oils for specific purposes. Not all oils blend well together, so careful selection is important.

Steps to Begin Blending:

1. Identify the issue(s) you want to address.
2. Select oils that target those specific concerns.
3. Check which oils blend well to create a broader healing base.
4. Always dilute essential oils with a carrier oil before applying them to the skin.

Applying Essential Oils to the Skin

Like most medicines, essential oils are metabolized quickly and do not remain in the body for long. To achieve maximum benefit:

- Reapply essential oils several times a day.
- When applied to the wrist, oils usually enter the bloodstream in about 20 seconds, take around 20 minutes to circulate throughout the body, and are then expelled. However, this timeline can vary from person to person.

Essential Oils with Skin-Healing Properties:

- Cedarwood
- Frankincense
- German Chamomile
- Geranium
- Helichrysum
- Jasmine
- Lavender
- Myrrh
- Neroli
- Patchouli
- Rose
- Sandalwood
- Vetiver
- Roman Chamomile
- Ylang-Ylang

Essential Oils and Allergies

Allergies are caused by histamine responses to triggers such as food, pollen, dust, or pet dander. Some people may also react negatively to essential oils, experiencing diarrhea, tongue swelling, sneezing, or wheezing. Some oils work to provide allergy relief.

Essential Oils for Allergy Relief:

- Elemi (Psoriasis)
- Eucalyptus (Sinus, Asthma)
- Lavender (Respiratory)
- Ledum (Digestive)
- Lemon (Pollen, Molds)
- Melissa (Skin)
- Patchouli (Vomiting, Cramps)
- Peppermint (Sinus)
- **Spikenard** (Sinus)

Diluting Essential Oils

The Alliance of International Aromatherapists (AIA) provides the following dilution guidelines:

2% dilution for the average adult with no known issues (3 drops essential oil per tablespoon carrier oil).

1% dilution for older adults (65+), children (age 6+), pregnant women, or individuals with sensitive skin or compromised immune systems.

Limonene: Benefits and Risks

Limonene, a terpene found in citrus fruits, has gained popularity in personal health. Research (PubMed.gov) highlights its potential therapeutic effects, including:

- Anti-inflammatory
- Antioxidant
- Anticancer
- Antidiabetic
- Gastroprotective

(Reference: Vieira AJ, Beserra FP, Souza MC, Totti BM, Rozza AL. *Limonene: Aroma of Innovation in Health and Disease.* Chem Biol Interact. 2018 Mar;283:97-106. DOI: 10.1016/j.cbi.2018.02.007.)

Recommended Dosage:

2 grams per day.

Megadoses (8+ grams daily) can cause nausea, vomiting, or skin irritation. Pregnant or breastfeeding women should consult a doctor before use.

Layering Essential Oils

Known as **Raindrop Therapy** or **Aroma Touch**, layering involves applying pure essential oils directly to the skin without carrier oils. Despite its popularity, this practice is controversial.

Professional aromatherapist organizations, such as the *Alliance of International Aromatherapists*, advise against Raindrop Therapy due to the potential for skin irritation and other adverse effects.

If you have concerns, consult your medical doctor. I recommend adding a carrier oil to the suggested essential oils to reduce potential skin irritation.

Ceremony in Layering

One criticism of Raindrop Therapy is its inclusion of ceremonial elements, which some consider unnecessary. However, I believe that ceremony can help clients relax and tune into the healing process. The 16th-century German proverb, *"Don't throw out the baby with the bath water,"* is fitting here. With adjustments, layering can be a beneficial and safe practice. Here is a ceremony for Layering Essential Oils.

Proposed Layering Ceremony

Creating sacred space is the first step. Smudge your treatment area by wafting burning White Sage or Pala Santo. Slowly walk around your area

Take a few minutes to clear away any negative energy you may have by doing 3-4 minutes of deep breathing, or do a 5-minute meditation. This is called 'grounding.'

Invite your client into the treatment space. Take a couple of minutes to waft burning White Sage or Pala Santo around the individual, going from the top of the head to the feet.

Turn on soft music and leave the room as the client removes their clothes and then lies face down on the massage table.

Cover the lower extremities of the client's body. Then ask the client to state their intention for the session. And as they do so, set your healing intention. (If this is a shamanic healing session, say, "Spirits, guide my hands as I lay on the layers of essential oils for (client's) greater benefit.

Recommended Practice

- Always **dilute essential oils** with a carrier oil before application.
- Conduct a **patch test** to check for adverse skin reactions.
- If you are a practitioner, ask your client about known essential or carrier oil allergies.

I recommend Jojoba Oil or Olive Oil for carrier oils, as they are less likely to trigger allergic reactions than nut-based oils.

Suggested Essential Oils for Layering

- **Holy Basil**
- **Wintergreen***
- **Marjoram**
- **Cypress**
- **Thyme**
- **Peppermint**

- **Oregano**
- **Cedarwood**
- **Lavender**
- **Ylang-Ylang**

*Wintergreen has been criticized for its potency, but research shows it is effective as a natural pain reliever. (Hebert PR, Barice EJ, Hennekens CH. *Treatment of low back pain: The potential clinical and public health benefits of topical herbal remedies.* J Altern Complement Med. 2014 Apr;20(4):219-20. DOI: 10.1089/acm... 2013.0313.)

Traditional Layering Technique for Back Pain

What You Will Need:

- **2 drops** of Holy Basil Essential Oil
- **3 drops** of Wintergreen Essential Oil
- **2 drops** of Marjoram Essential Oil
- **1 drop** of Cypress Essential Oil
- **1 drop** of Thyme Essential Oil
- **2 drops** of Peppermint Essential Oil
- **1 drop** of Oregano Essential Oil
- **2 drops** of Cedarwood Essential Oil
- **2 drops** of Lavender Essential Oil
- **2 drops** of Ylang-Ylang Essential Oil
- **A large warmed bath towel**

Directions for Traditional Layering:

Begin at the base of the spine with Holy Basil and add a new oil as you move up the spine. Take your time. Give the oil a chance to soak into the skin. Cover the client's back with the warmed bath towel.

Give the client 15 minutes, then you step out and have the client get dressed.

Alternate Layering Technique

- **2 ounces** of Jojoba Oil (or preferred carrier oil)
- A sterilized dark brown bottle with an eye dropper
- 2 drops of each of the recommended oils
- A large, warmed bath towel

Directions:

1. **Mix the Oils**: Combine the essential oils with the carrier oil in the sterilized bottle. Shake thoroughly.
2. **Prepare the Towel**: Warm the towel and place it over the shoulders or lower back.
3. **Apply the Oil**: Dispense a small amount of the oil mixture and apply it to the affected area. Do **not** rub it in.
4. **Relax**: Leave the oil on for 20 minutes while the towel remains in place.

For Essential Oil Practitioners:

- Ensure the client is comfortable on a massage table with adequate head and neck support.
- Check for residual oil at the end of 20 minutes and gently massage the area if needed.
- Pat the skin dry with a clean towel.

CHAPTER SIX

Shamanic Meditation & Essential Oils

"Mindfulness allows us to become keen observers of ourselves and gradually transform the way our minds operate." – Mark W. Muesse, Ph.D.

The Origins of Meditation

The early records of meditation are scarce, making it difficult to trace its exact origins. However, some evidence suggests that meditation may have been practiced as part of the Vedic tradition, which originated in what is now Iran around 1500 BCE. The Chinese Taoists and Indian Buddhists also developed distinct forms of meditation by the 6th century BCE, though historical accounts vary. The complex history of meditation is further obscured by its many forms, each rooted in different cultural and religious traditions.

In the Western world, interest in meditation grew in the 1700s CE when European translations of Eastern philosophy texts introduced the concept of meditation. However, it was Swami Vivekananda's presence at the Parliament of Religions in Chicago in 1893 that sparked widespread fascination with Eastern meditation practices. His teachings influenced many other prominent Indian spiritual leaders, such as Swami Rama, Mukunda Lal Ghosh, and Maharishi Mahesh Yogi, who helped establish meditation as a popular practice in the United States during the 20th century.

Popular Types of Meditation

Over the centuries, meditation has evolved into many different forms, each designed to achieve various mental, emotional, and spiritual goals. Some of the most widely practiced types include:

- Mindfulness Meditation
- Spiritual Meditation
- Focused Meditation
- Movement Meditation
- Mantra Meditation
- Transcendental Meditation
- Progressive Relaxation
- Loving-Kindness Meditation

This chapter focuses on **Mindfulness Meditation**, one of the most well-known and practiced forms of meditation worldwide.

Mindfulness Meditations trace back to ancient India, around 1500 BCE, within the context of the early Hindu practice of yoga. Initially, yoga emphasized stillness and breathing instead of the physical postures and movements commonly associated with yoga today. The core of mindfulness meditation focuses on awareness, presence, and the stillness of both body and mind.

In the 1970s, **Jon Kabat-Zinn** founded the Stress Reduction Clinic at the University of Massachusetts Medical School, where he introduced mindfulness meditation to Western medicine. Over time, it became a widely accepted practice, especially for reducing stress, anxiety, and depression. Mindfulness also helps people cultivate emotional resilience, fostering an enhanced ability to navigate the complexities of daily life.

The three foundational principles of mindfulness meditation are:

1. **Setting the intention** to cultivate awareness.
2. **Paying attention** to the present moment without judgment, simply as an observer.
3. **Adopting a non-judgmental attitude** toward whatever arises during meditation.

On a personal note, I began my meditation journey following the teachings of **Maharishi Mahesh Yogi** and later, the philosophical insights of the late **Alan Watts**. Eventually, I found my way into mindfulness meditation, influenced by the teachings of **Mark W. Muesse**, whose approach is deeply rooted in **Vipassana meditation**, one of India's oldest meditative traditions.

One of the most significant lessons meditation teaches is a deeper awareness of our breath. This simple yet profound practice helps us better understand our body, relax our mind, and may even improve overall well-being. It is this awareness of the breath that forms the foundation of both mindfulness meditation and shamanic meditation, which we will now explore in more detail.

Shamanic Meditation vs. Shamanic Journeying

Shamanic practices can be divided into two primary types:

Shamanic Meditation and **Shamanic Journeying**. While both practices involve entering altered states of consciousness, their purposes and methods differ.

- **Shamanic Meditation** is intended to re-energize and restore the individual by facilitating a heightened state of presence in the "eternal now."
- **Shamanic Journeying**, on the other hand, is a technique used to connect with the Spirit World for healing, guidance, or insight

Shamanic Meditation: The Practice

In traditional shamanic cultures, healers often meditated outdoors, allowing the natural world's rhythms to guide them into stillness. While this may not be feasible for most people in today's busy world, the principles of shamanic meditation remain universally accessible.

The goal of shamanic meditation is not to concentrate on a single thought or idea, but rather to quiet the mind and attune yourself to a higher state of awareness. The practice encourages presence in the moment, helping you to move beyond mental distractions.

Getting Ready for Shamanic Meditation

1. **Find a Comfortable Space:** Choose a quiet room where you can relax, lower the lights, and create a

calming environment. A dimly lit room is ideal, though total darkness is not recommended unless you're preparing for sleep.
2. **Choose the Right Seating:** While the traditional seated position (such as yoga pose) is effective, you may prefer to sit in a comfortable chair. Avoid lying down, as this increases the likelihood of falling asleep.
3. **Select a Sound for Meditation:** Background sound can support the meditation experience. Choose something soothing. Consider these apps: Inner Timer, Calm, Spotify, or YouTube. Also, consider these tracks: Deuter, Liquid Mind, Meditative Mind, or Anugama.

4. **Use for Essential Oils:** Scent can profoundly influence the meditative experience. Select an essential oil known for its calming and grounding properties. Here are two recipes for your consideration:

Recipe One

Ingredients:

3 drops of Frankincense. It promotes spiritual connection and mental clarity
2 drops of Lavender. It calms the mind and reduces stress
2 drops of Cedarwood. It grounds and centers your energy
2 drops of Bergamot. It uplifts your mood while keeping you calm

Directions for use:

Add the oils to a diffuser and run it in your meditation space, or mix these oils with 10 ml of a carrier oil such as jojoba. Apply two drops to your wrists and rub them together for 20 seconds, or place a drop behind each ear.

Recipe Two

Ingredients:

4 drops of Sandalwood. It encourages a deep meditative state
3 drops of Peppermint. It clears the mind and boosts alertness
2 drops of Lemon. Invigorates and sharpens focus
1 drop of Ylang-Ylang. It balances your emotions.,

Directions:

Add the oils to a diffuser or mix the oils and add them to a roll-on. If you use a roll-on, apply the oils to the back of the neck.

The Meditation Process

1. Get Comfortable: Sit in a comfortable chair or position with your hands resting on your lap, and palms facing upward. Gently connect the index finger and thumb of each hand, forming a circle.

2. Breathe with Intention: Begin by taking five slow, deep breaths using the Ujjayi breath technique (a form of controlled breathing often used in yoga). Allow your breath to center you and calm your mind.

3. Set Your Intention: Reflect on why you are meditating. Set an intention, whether for relaxation, healing, or personal clarity

4. Breathe and Relax: Continue breathing deeply and naturally. As you settle into the practice, allow your body to relax with each exhale, letting go of tension in your muscles and mind.

5. Conclude the Session: After 10 to 15 minutes, gently bring the meditation to a close. Slowly rise from your seated position, stretching your arms overhead to ground yourself. Take a few deep breaths and drink some water to help rehydrate and restore energy.

Remember, practice makes perfect. The more consistently you meditate, the more profound the benefits will become.

May you find peace, clarity, and healing through your practice of shamanic meditation. Namaste.

CHAPTER SEVEN

Essential Oils for the Bedroom

In previous chapters, we've explored two primary methods of using essential oils: **Topical Application** and **Inhalation**. Recently, there has been growing interest in a third method—**ingestion**. However, it's important to note that the ingestion of essential oils can be **hazardous** and potentially fatal. I recommend that you **never ingest pure essential oils**, and if you are considering this method, always dilute them significantly in water under the guidance of a trained professional. AND before that, talk to your doctor!

As we continue to explore the various applications of essential oils, remember that some oils, especially those used to influence mood and emotions, require extra caution.

Mood is a conscious state of mind, often linked to predominant emotions or feelings. The eight basic emotions are generally considered to be joy, sadness, fear, anger, surprise, disgust, trust, and anticipation.

Sexual Desire: A crucial emotion often overlooked in emotional wellness discussions is **sexual desire**. This aspect of intimacy plays a significant role in personal well-being, yet sexual dysfunction is more common than many realize. Studies show that **43% of women** and **31% of men** experience some form of sexual dysfunction, with erectile dysfunction (ED) affecting most men by the age of 45. It's predicted that by 2025, **322 million men worldwide** will experience ED, contributing to an annual economic impact of over $2 billion. While various treatments, including pharmaceutical interventions, exist, these may not always be affordable or suitable for everyone.

So, what options are available for those seeking a natural alternative to support intimacy and emotional connection? This is where **essential oils** can offer potential benefits. There are essential oils that may help support sexual health and restore intimacy for both women and men dealing with sexual dysfunction.

Six Essential Oils for Intimacy and Sexual Health

The following oils have been chosen for their known aphrodisiac properties and ability to support sexual health, including helping to alleviate issues like **erectile dysfunction** and promoting a deeper emotional connection.

1. **Catuaba**
2. **Clary Sage**
3. **Davana**
4. **Neroli**
5. **Patchouli**
6. **Ylang-Ylang**

Catuaba

Catuaba is an essential oil derived from the bark of trees found in the **Brazilian rainforest**. It is well known for its ability to stimulate the nervous system and may promote an **erection** in men. As an aphrodisiac, Catuaba is also used for a range of other health benefits, including:

Anxiety relief

- **Asthma management**
- **Bacterial infections**
- **Bronchitis**
- **Depression**
- **Fatigue**
- **Insomnia**
- **Memory enhancement**

Catuaba can be found in various forms, such as capsules, extracts, powders, and bark. Dosages typically range from **375 to 475 mg**, depending on the manufacturer. **Do not exceed the recommended dose**, and always consult with a healthcare professional before use.

If you're using **Catuaba bark** (wildcrafted), please ensure you **boil the bark** and steep it for **15 minutes** to reduce any potential contaminants.

Caution: While Catuaba can be effective, it may cause side effects such as headaches, dizziness, rapid heart rate, and in some cases, priapism (prolonged erections). Women should not use Catuaba as it may impair fertility, and it should not be given to children.

Clary Sage

Not to be confused with the culinary sage, **Clary Sage** is an essential oil extracted from the leaves and flower buds of the **Salvia sclarea** plant. Known as "The Woman's Oil," Clary Sage is especially beneficial for female health but also offers a variety of general wellness uses, including:

Skin wound healing
Depression relief

Hot flash reduction
Menstrual cramp alleviation
Libido Stress reduction and enhancement

How to Use Clary Sage Essential Oil:

Inhalation: Place the bottle near your nose and inhale deeply several times to help calm anxiety or stress.

Room Spray: Add **3-5 drops** of Clary Sage to a spray bottle filled with **1 cup of water**. Shake the mixture well and spritz it around the room to promote a calming environment.

Bedding & Closet Freshener: Lightly spritz your bedding and closets with the Clary Sage spray to create a serene, romantic atmosphere.

Menstrual Cramp Relief:

Combine **3-5 drops** of Clary Sage with **10-15 drops of carrier oil**. Warm the mixture and massage it gently into your abdomen daily to help ease menstrual discomfort.

Hot Flash Relief: Add **2-3 drops** to a carrier oil and massage into your feet to reduce hot flashes associated with menopause.

Caution: Those with low blood pressure should avoid using Clary Sage Essential Oil.

Davana Essential Oil

Native to **India**, **Davana** is a member of the daisy family and is often used for its rich, warm, and slightly sweet aroma. Davana Essential Oil is especially beneficial for:

- Bacterial infections
- Bronchial congestion
- Calming nervous stomachs
- Relieving menstrual cramps
- Reducing anxiety, stress, and tension
- Enhancing skin appearance
- Aphrodisiac effects

Davana can help set a romantic mood and support intimacy in the following ways:

Massage: Combine **12 drops of Davana Essential Oil** with **1 oz of carrier oil**. Have your partner massage your shoulders and back to help relax and spark arousal.

Mood Setting: Add **4 drops of Davana** to a diffuser to create an inviting and romantic atmosphere.

Body Application: Blend **2-4 drops of** Davana Essential Oil with your choice of carrier oil.

Apply 1 drop behind each ear and 1 drop at the neckline for a subtle, alluring effect.

Conclusion: Harnessing Essential Oils for Intimacy and Emotional Wellness

Incorporating essential oils into your bedroom routine offers a natural and holistic approach to supporting intimacy and sexual wellness. While essential oils can significantly enhance mood, relaxation, and libido, always use them safely and responsibly.

It's important to remember that **essential oils are powerful** and should be treated with care, especially when applied to the skin or used in your environment. Always consult a healthcare professional if you have concerns, especially if you are pregnant, nursing, or have pre-existing health conditions.

By using these essential oils thoughtfully, you can help promote better physical well-being and a deeper emotional connection with your partner.

Neroli Essential Oil

Neroli Essential Oil is derived from French Orange Blossoms through steam distillation. This oil is highly regarded for its therapeutic and aromatic properties, serving as an antidepressant, aphrodisiac, and antiseptic. It is known to impact the following positively:

- Soothing the nervous system
- Releasing tension
- Relieving anxiety
- Increasing circulation
- Uplifting mood
- Boosting libido
- Reducing frigidity
- Addressing erectile dysfunction

How to Use Neroli Essential Oil to Enhance Your Love Life

1. **Aromatherapy**: Add 3 to 4 drops of Neroli Essential Oil to a diffuser and let it run for 20 minutes before bedtime. The calming and uplifting aroma creates a relaxing atmosphere.
2. **Massage**: Mix 3 to 4 drops of Neroli Essential Oil with 8 ounces of Sweet Almond Oil or another carrier oil of your choice. Warm the mixture slightly, then use it for a slow, circular massage on your partner to promote relaxation and intimacy.

Patchouli Essential Oil

Patchouli Essential Oil is extracted from the dried leaves of the Patchouli plant through a distillation process. It offers a wide range of benefits, including:

- Treating dermatitis, acne, and dry skin
- Easing symptoms of colds, headaches, and stomach issues
- Relieving depression
- Reducing stress and anxiety
- Controlling appetite
- Boosting libido

How to Use Patchouli Essential Oil

For Skin Issues:

Dry Skin: Mix 1-2 drops of Patchouli Essential Oil with a carrier oil like Sweet Almond Oil and apply to the affected area.

Acne: Combine 1-2 drops of Patchouli Essential Oil with Grapeseed Oil and dab it on the acne spots.

As an Aphrodisiac:

Patchouli Essential Oil enhances libido by stimulating estrogen and testosterone production while reducing sexual anxiety. To use:

Combine 1-2 drops of Patchouli Essential Oil with a thick carrier oil such as Hempseed Oil.

Warm the mixture slightly and give your partner a relaxing massage.

Safety Precautions

Patchouli Essential Oil is generally safe for use, but keep these points in mind:

Always perform a patch test before application.

Never apply undiluted oil directly to the skin.

If using a diffuser, ensure the area is well-ventilated to avoid headaches, nausea, or dizziness.

Do not use on young children.

Ylang-Ylang Essential Oil

Ylang-Ylang Essential Oil is produced by distilling the flowers of the Ylang-Ylang tree, often referred to as the "flower of flowers." Approximately 200 pounds of flowers are required to produce one liter of essential oil. Ylang-Ylang is renowned for its diverse benefits:

- Boosting self-esteem
- Calming the mind
- Releasing anger
- Relieving tension
- Soothing and moisturizing the skin
- Hydrating hair

Aphrodisiac Properties

Ylang-Ylang Essential Oil is one of the most potent natural aphrodisiacs. It increases libido, enhances physical attraction, and promotes circulation and energy.

Recipe for Ylang-Ylang Sensual Massage

Ingredients:

- Ylang-Ylang Essential Oil
- Sandalwood Essential Oil
- Jasmine Grandiflorum Absolute

- Your preferred carrier oil (e.g., Sweet Almond Oil, Jojoba Oil)
- 1 sterilized small glass bottle
- 1 sterilized eyedropper

Directions:

Combine 6 drops of Ylang-Ylang Essential Oil, 4 drops of Sandalwood Essential Oil, and 2 drops of Jasmine Grandiflorum Absolute in the sterilized glass bottle.

Add 2 ounces of your preferred carrier oil to the mixture.

Close the bottle tightly and shake gently to mix.

Use the eyedropper to dispense a small amount of the blend onto your hands and warm it slightly before applying.

> Massage your partner gently in slow, circular motions to encourage relaxation and intimacy

*****

Incorporating these essential oils into your routine can create a more soothing and sensual environment while enjoying their therapeutic benefits.

Here is a wonderful source on blending Essential Oils: *Essential Oil Complimentary Blending Chart*, created by Melody Joy Elick. It's available as a download, as a PDF, or as a TXT. It is also available online to be read on Scribd.

CHAPTER EIGHT

Essential Oils For Alopecia Areata Hair Loss, And Neuropathy

What is Alopecia Areata? Alopecia Areata is a disease that occurs when the immune system mistakenly attacks hair follicles, leading to hair loss. This autoimmune condition affects nearly 8 million Americans and approximately 2% of the global population. Individuals with autoimmune disorders such as psoriasis, thyroid disease, or vitiligo are at an increased risk of developing Alopecia Areata.

The severity of Alopecia Areata varies significantly among individuals. Some may experience intermittent episodes of hair loss throughout their lives. While there is currently no cure for the disease, various treatments and natural remedies can help manage symptoms and reduce its impact. Below is a guide to essential oils known for their effectiveness in mitigating hair loss.

Recommended Essential Oils For Alopecia and General Hair Loss

Black Pepper	Cedarwood	Clary Sage
Clove	Cypress	Frankincense
Geranium	Chamomile	Ginger
Lavender	Lemon	Mastic
Palmarosa	Rosemary	Rosewood
Sage	Sandalwood	Spikenard

Thyme   Ylang-Ylang

Recipes For Alopecia and Hair Loss

Recipe #1:

Hair Regrowth Blend

What You Will Need:

1 60ml (3 oz) dark-colored glass bottle with stopper
20 drops of Cedarwood essential oil
20 drops of Lavender essential oil
20 drops of Rosemary essential oil
Carrier oil of your choice (e.g., jojoba, sweet almond, or coconut oil)

Directions:

1. Sterilize the glass bottle and eyedropper to ensure cleanliness.
2. Add all the essential oils (Cedarwood, Lavender, Thyme, and Rosemary) to the bottle.
3. Fill the rest of the bottle with the carrier oil, leaving a small space at the top for the stopper.
4. Secure the stopper and gently shake the bottle to thoroughly mix the ingredients.

How to Use:

1. Apply 2 to 4 drops of the blend to areas of hair loss.

2. Gently massage the oil into the scalp, focusing on affected areas.
3. Perform this treatment at night to allow maximum absorption. Wash your hair in the morning using a mild shampoo.
4. Repeat this process three times a week for three weeks, then take a one-week break. Resume the routine as needed until satisfactory hair growth is achieved. Over time, you may need to repeat the process intermittently to maintain results.

Tips for Maximizing Results:

- Always conduct a patch test before using any new essential oil.
- Maintain a balanced diet rich in vitamins and minerals that support hair health.
- Incorporate stress-reducing activities like yoga or meditation, as stress can exacerbate hair loss.
- Combine the use of essential oils with other treatments as recommended by a healthcare professional.

Note: While essential oils may be effective in managing hair loss, results may vary, and it is important to consult a medical professional for a comprehensive treatment plan tailored to your individual needs. It takes time. Be patient.

NEUROPATHY AND ESSENTIAL OILS

Neuropathy occurs when your nerves stop functioning properly, often due to damage or destruction of nerve cells. Symptoms may include pain, tingling, or weakness in the feet, legs, and hands. It may also cause changes in gait or mobility. Approximately 60% to 70% of individuals with diabetes experience neuropathy.

Common Causes of Neuropathy:

1. Autoimmune diseases
2. Diabetes
3. Infections
4. Inherited conditions
5. Tumors
6. Bone marrow disorders
7. Vitamin B12 deficiency
8. Excessive Vitamin B6

Note: This information is intended to complement, not replace, traditional medical treatments. It is all about incorporating essential oils into your regimen.

Recommended Essential Oils for Neuropathy Relief

The following essential oils are known to provide relief for neuropathy symptoms:

- Bergamot
- Cinnamon
- Eucalyptus
- Geranium
- Ginger
- Helichrysum
- Holy Basil
- Lavender
- Lemongrass

- Peppermint
- Tea Tree

Recipes for the treatment of Neuropathy:

Here are recipes for managing neuropathy using essential oils. Each recipe focuses on a blend of oils with therapeutic properties that may help alleviate symptoms such as pain, numbness, and tingling.

Bergamot Essential Oil for Calming Nerves in feet, legs, and hands

Ingredients:

5 drops of Bergamot Essential Oil
2 drops of Frankincense Essential Oil
2 drops of Chamomile Essential Oil
1 ounce of Sweet Almond Oil. For those who may have negative reactions to nuts, use Jojoba Oil.

Directions:

Thoroughly mix the oils. Pour them into a small dark bottle with a top.

Apply a small amount of the mixture to the leg(s), foot (feet), and or hand (s) two times a day.

Important Note: Bergamot is photosensitive; you should avoid sun exposure for 12 hours. Consider using bergapten-free; the FCF version if you have concerns about photosensitivity.

Cinnamon Essential Oil as a Circulation Booster

Ingredients:
2 drops of Cinnamon Leaf Essential Oil*
3 drops of Ginger Essential Oil
2 drops of Black Pepper Essential Oil
1 ounce of Coconut Oil or Jojoba Oil

Directions:
Mix the oils.
Apply a little to the numb areas. Do this twice a day: once in the morning and at bedtime.
*Cinnamon Leaf is not as strong as Cinnamon Bark; therefore, there is less chance of skin irritation

Eucalyptus Essential Oil for Nerve Repair

Ingredients:

6 drops of Eucalyptus Essential Oil
3 drops of Peppermint Essential Oil
3drops of Tea Tree Essential Oil
1 ounce of Aloe Vera Gel

Directions:
Mix the ingredients,
Apply to the inflamed area.
Important Note: Avoid applying this mixture to broken skin.

Geranium, Tea Tree, and Peppermint Soothing Oil Blend

These oils have anti-inflammatory, analgesic, and circulation-boosting properties, which may help soothe neuropathy-related discomfort.

Ingredients:

- 5 drops of Geranium essential oil
- 5 drops of Tea Tree essential oil
- 5 drops of Peppermint essential oil
- 2 tablespoons of carrier oil (such as coconut oil or jojoba oil)

Directions:

1. In a small glass container, combine the Geranium, Tea Tree, and Peppermint oils.
2. Add the carrier oil to dilute the essential oils.
3. Gently shake or stir to mix the oils.
4. Massage a small amount of the blend onto the affected areas 2-3 times daily, focusing on areas with nerve pain or discomfort.
5. Store in a cool, dark place.

Ginger, Holy Basil, and Lavender Relaxing Balm

Ginger and Holy Basil are known for their anti-inflammatory and nerve-calming effects, while Lavender provides soothing properties. This balm can help relax tense muscles and ease nerve discomfort.

Ingredients:

- 4 drops of Ginger essential oil
- 4 drops of Holy Basil essential oil
- 6 drops of Lavender essential oil
- 2 tablespoons of beeswax (for balm consistency)
- 2 tablespoons of carrier oil (such as sweet almond oil)

Directions:

1. In a double boiler, melt the beeswax and carrier oil together, stirring until smooth.
2. Remove from heat and add the Ginger, Holy Basil, and Lavender oils.
3. Stir well to combine.
4. Pour the mixture into a small glass jar or container and allow it to cool and solidify.
5. Apply the balm to affected areas once or twice a day, massaging gently to promote relaxation and pain relief.

Liquid Stitches and the Regeneration of the Nerves

Liquid Stitches, as Helichrysum is often called, is undoubtedly one of the most highly valued and respected oils. Its powerful, regenerative, and anti-inflammatory qualities make it a natural oil to help reduce the discomfort created by neuropathy.

Ingredients:

5 drops of Helichrysum essential oil
2 drops of Frankincense essential oil,
3 drops of Lavender Essential Oil
2 ounces of St. John's Wort-Infused oil, or use Jojoba oil,

Directions:
To thoroughly mix the oils, place the oils in a small dark bottle and shake.
Apply two drops to the affected leg and gently massage.
Do this when you get up in the morning and again when you retire.
Note: To be effective, use this for several weeks. Infused St. John's Wort Oil is helpful for nerve pain and inflammation.

Peppermint, Ginger, and Lavender Nerve Relief Massage Oil

This blend combines the cooling effect of Peppermint with the warming and anti-inflammatory properties of Ginger and the calming influence of Lavender, making it a great option for easing nerve discomfort.

Ingredients:

- 5 drops of Peppermint essential oil
- 5 drops of Ginger essential oil
- 5 drops of Lavender essential oil
- 2 tablespoons of carrier oil (such as grapeseed oil or olive oil)

Directions:

1. In a small container, combine the Peppermint, Ginger, and Lavender essential oils.
2. Add the carrier oil and mix well.
3. Massage the blend onto affected areas, using circular motions to improve circulation and promote relaxation.
4. Repeat as needed, especially after a long day or when symptoms flare up.

Notes:

- Always do a patch test before applying any blend to ensure you don't have a sensitivity or allergic reaction.
- If you have any existing health conditions, check with a healthcare provider before using essential oils.
- If you're pregnant or nursing, consult your doctor before using essential oils.

CHAPTER NINE

Essential Oils For Vertigo

It is estimated that 40% of adults in the United States suffer from vertigo at least once. With the current population of the United States at 332 million, this means that approximately 133 million individuals experience vertigo at some point in their lives.

Recognized as an inner ear disorder in the 1860s by a French doctor named Prosper Ménière (pronounced men-EARS), his last name became the technical term for the condition, which we now commonly refer to as vertigo.

Vertigo is described as a sensation of dizziness, unsteadiness, or balance issues. It is often caused by an inner ear infection. Vestibular neuritis, for example, may start after a cold. Vertigo affects people differently, ranging from mild to severe, with symptoms that may include:

- A sensation of pressure in the ears
- Migraine headaches
- Sweating
- Nausea and vomiting
- Anxiety
- Uncontrollable jerking of the eyes (nystagmus)

However, neuro-otologist Dr. Diego Kaski suggests that the general descriptors of vertigo may sometimes be mislabeled. He points out that many cases may be benign paroxysmal positional vertigo (BPPV).

Understanding Benign Paroxysmal Positional Vertigo (BPPV)

BPPV is triggered by specific changes in head position, such as tipping the head up or down. Vestibular migraines, another related condition, cause episodes of dizziness that may feel like rocking, spinning, floating, swaying, internal motion, or lightheadedness. Unlike some other medical conditions, vertigo does not cause loss of consciousness but can lead to falls and injuries.

BPPV is essentially a mechanical problem within the inner ear. The balance organs in the inner ear contain small crystals that move in response to motion. When these crystals become dislodged or misaligned, they can create the illusion of physical movement. Correcting this issue may require a head and neck adjustment performed by a qualified healthcare professional. Attempting such adjustments yourself is not recommended.

Types of Vertigo

There are three main types of vertigo:

1. **Objective Vertigo**: The sensation that the environment is in motion.
2. **Subjective Vertigo**: The sensation that the individual is in motion.
3. **Rotational Vertigo**: The sensation of spinning.

Medical Interventions

Medical doctors may prescribe specific medications, recommend dietary changes, or suggest exercise routines to help manage vertigo. However, for those seeking alternative remedies, essential oils have been recognized as effective in reducing the negative impact of vertigo.

Essential Oils for Vertigo

Before using any essential oils, consult with your medical doctor to ensure safety and compatibility with your health condition. The following essential oils are widely recognized for their effectiveness in both treating and preventing vertigo:

1. **Ginger Essential Oil**:

Mix 5 drops of ginger essential oil with 2 ounces of carrier oil.

Apply a small amount gently to your temples, chest, and the back of your neck.

Alternatively, add 3 drops to a diffuser, sit nearby, and breathe slowly.

2. **Cypress Essential Oil**:

Improves blood flow, enhances brain function, and reduces lightheadedness.

Add 3 to 5 drops to a room diffuser or boiling water for steam inhalation. Breathe deeply for 5 to 6 minutes.

Mix 5 drops with 2 ounces of carrier oil and use it as a chest rub before bedtime.

3. **Basil Essential Oil:**

This oil is effective when used in an inhaler or diffuser. Its anti-inflammatory and antioxidant properties help balance the nerves and calm the mind.

Follow the device's instructions: add 2 to 3 drops to an inhaler or up to 5 drops to a diffuser. Start the diffuser 5 to 10 minutes before retiring.

4. **Eucalyptus Essential Oil:**

Helps reduce sinus pressure and can be used in an inhaler or diffuser.

Mixed with carrier oil, it can be applied directly to the chest, temples, or forehead.

Other essential oils that may help reduce the symptoms of vertigo include:

- Clary Sage
- Frankincense
- Rosemary
- Lavender
- Peppermint
- Rose Oil

Additional Essential Oil Recipes for Vertigo

Here are some recipes that include Clary Sage, Frankincense, Rosemary, Lavender,

Calming Blend for Vertigo:

Rub 2 drops of Clary Sage into the temples, back of the neck, and wrists.

Grounding Diffuser Blend:

3 drops Frankincense
2 drops Rosemary
1 drop Peppermint

Add the oils to a diffuser with water as per the device's instructions. Use in a quiet space to help alleviate dizziness.

Steam Inhalation Recipe:

2 drops Rosemary
2 drops Eucalyptus
1 drop of Clary Sage

Add these oils to a bowl of steaming water, lean over the bowl, place a towel over your head, and inhale deeply for 5 minutes.

Refreshing Roller Blend:

3 drops Peppermint
2 drops Lavender
1 drop of Rose Oil

Combine in a 10 mL roller bottle with carrier oil. Roll onto pulse points as needed for relief.

By incorporating these essential oils into your wellness routine, you may find relief from vertigo symptoms while promoting overall balance and well-being.

CHAPTER TEN

Advanced Essential Oil Recipes For Vertigo Relief

Building on the foundational knowledge of essential oils for vertigo, this module focuses on advanced blends and targeted applications. The recipes below incorporate essential oils like Clary Sage, Frankincense, Rosemary, Lavender, Peppermint, and Rose Oil to provide a comprehensive approach to managing vertigo symptoms.

Understanding the Benefits of Specific Oils

- **Clary Sage**: Known for its calming properties, it helps reduce stress and balances the nervous system.
- **Frankincense**: Improves focus, reduces anxiety, and enhances grounding.
- **Rosemary**: Stimulates circulation and sharpens mental clarity.
- **Lavender**: Soothes headaches and promotes relaxation.
- **Peppermint**: Alleviates nausea and enhances alertness.
- **Rose Oil**: Provides a calming effect and reduces tension.

Recipes for Vertigo Relief

1. Soothing Massage Blend

This blend promotes relaxation and eases dizziness.

- 3 drops Clary Sage
- 2 drops Lavender
- 1 drop Rose Oil
- 2 ounces carrier oil (e.g., coconut or almond oil)

Instructions: Mix the essential oils with the carrier oil thoroughly. Gently massage the blend onto the temples, back of the neck, and shoulders. Use circular motions to enhance absorption and relaxation.

2. Grounding Aromatherapy Diffuser Blend

Ideal for creating a calming environment that helps stabilize vertigo symptoms.

- 2 drops Frankincense
- 2 drops Rosemary
- 1 drop Lavender
- 1 drop Peppermint

Instructions: Add the oils to your diffuser with the appropriate amount of water as directed. Use in a quiet space and breathe deeply for 10-15 minutes.

3. Cooling Roll-On Remedy

Perfect for on-the-go relief from sudden dizziness or nausea.

- 3 drops Peppermint
- 2 drops Lavender
- 2 drops Clary Sage
- 10 mL roller bottle
- Carrier oil (e.g., jojoba or fractionated coconut oil)

Instructions: Combine the essential oils in the roller bottle and fill the rest with the carrier oil. Shake well before use. Apply to pulse points, such as the wrists and behind the ears.

4. Invigorating Steam Inhalation

This recipe helps clear the sinuses and enhances circulation, reducing vertigo symptoms.

- 2 drops Rosemary
- 2 drops Eucalyptus
- 1 drop Frankincense
- Bowl of steaming hot water

Instructions: Add the essential oils to the bowl of hot water. Place a towel over your head to create a tent and inhale deeply for 5-7 minutes. Avoid getting too close to the steam to prevent burns.

5. Calming Bath Soak

Relax and unwind while reducing vertigo symptoms with this therapeutic bath soak.

- 4 drops Lavender
- 3 drops Clary Sage
- 2 drops Rose Oil
- 1 cup Epsom salt

Instructions: Mix the essential oils with the Epsom salt. Add the mixture to a warm bath and stir to dissolve. Soak for 20-30 minutes to enjoy the full benefits.

6. Balancing Mist Spray

Use this spray to refresh your senses and reduce dizziness.

- 3 drops Frankincense
- 3 drops Peppermint
- 2 drops Lavender
- 4 ounces distilled water
- 1 teaspoon witch hazel (optional, as an emulsifier)
- Spray bottle

Instructions: Combine the essential oils, witch hazel, and water in the spray bottle. Shake well before each use. Mist around your face and neck, avoiding direct contact with the eyes.

By incorporating these recipes into your daily routine, you can create a multifaceted approach to managing vertigo. Whether through massage, aromatherapy, or topical applications, these blends offer natural and effective support for balance and well-being.

Please remember, these oils are not a replacement for medical treatment. They are supportive.

CHAPTER ELEVEN

The Hypothalamus, Thyroid, And Essential Oils

The hypothalamus is a structure deep within the brain, about the size of a pearl. It serves as the main link between the endocrine and nervous systems, producing hormones that regulate body temperature, heart rate, and hunger. It also communicates with the thyroid through the Hypothalamic-Pituitary-Thyroid Axis, a critical feedback loop for maintaining balance in the body. Chronic stress can disrupt this communication, leading to physical, mental, and emotional health issues.

Five highly recommended essential oils for easing stress and supporting hypothalamic balance are: **Frankincense**, **Mandarin**, **Patchouli**, **Pine**, and **Ylang-Ylang**. These oils can be used in roll-on bottles or sprays. If only one oil is available, **Frankincense Essential Oil** is highly recommended.

Essential Oil Recipe for the Hypothalamus

Roll-On Bottle Recipe

Ingredients:

- 5 drops of Frankincense Essential Oil
- 2 drops of Mandarin Essential Oil
- 2 drops of Patchouli Essential Oil
- 3 drops of Pine Essential Oil
- 2 drops of Ylang-Ylang Essential Oil
- 20 drops of carrier oil (e.g., Sweet Almond Oil

Instructions:

- Add all ingredients to a roll-on bottle.
- Insert the roller ball, secure the cap, and shake well.
- Apply four rolls to the Third Eye (just above the nose, between the eyebrows).
- Gently massage the area to help the oils absorb. Use daily, preferably at bedtime.

Spray Bottle Recipe:

- **Ingredients**:
- 5 drops of Frankincense Essential Oil
- 20 drops of carrier oil
- **Instructions**:
    1. Mix the oils thoroughly in a spray bottle.
    2. Spray a small amount onto one hand and gently massage the center of the forehead.
    3. Use daily, ideally before bedtime.

The Thyroid

The thyroid is a small gland located in the front of the throat, just below the Adam's apple and above the collarbone. It regulates metabolism—the conversion of oxygen and food into cellular energy. Thyroid issues are common, with two primary types: *Hypothyroidism* (Underactive thyroid) and *Hyperthyroidism* (Overactive thyroid).

Hypothyroidism

Symptoms:

- Cold hands and feet
- Constipation
- Difficulty losing weight
- Fatigue
- Heavy menstrual periods
- Lack of initiative
- Sleepiness even after a full night's sleep

Essential Oils for Hypothyroidism:

- Clove
- Ledum
- Myrrh
- Peppermint
- Rose Geranium
- Cedarwood

Ledum Essential Oil: Ledum (Greenland Moss or Labrador Tea) has been valued for centuries for its medicinal properties. It helps regulate hormone levels and supports healthy metabolic function.

Recommended Dosage for Hypothyroidism

- **General Use:**
- 1 drop of essential oil mixed with a carrier oil, tea, honey, toast, or water.

- **Examples**:
- Add 1 drop of oil to a cup of hot tea.
- Place 1 drop on a teaspoon of honey, ensuring the oil doesn't touch your lips.
- Add 1 drop to a piece of toast or a quarter glass of water.

Note: Always consult a medical doctor before using essential oils for thyroid issues to avoid conflicts with existing treatments.

Hyperthyroidism

Symptoms:

- Weight loss
- Irregular heartbeat
- Muscle weakness
- Enlarged thyroid (goiter)

Hyperthyroidism can also lead to difficulty breathing or swallowing due to an enlarged thyroid gland.

Essential Oils for Hyperthyroidism:

- Lemongrass
- Frankincense
- Lavender
- Wintergreen
- Sandalwood
- Pine

While essential oils cannot stop the overproduction of thyroid hormones, they may alleviate symptoms. Use methods similar to those for hypothyroidism.

Using essential oils for hypothyroidism can provide benefits, including supporting emotional well-being, reducing stress, and promoting relaxation. Here are some recipes utilizing the essential oils you mentioned:

1. Thyroid Support Aromatherapy Roll-On

This roll-on blend can be used to support overall thyroid health by stimulating the body's energy flow and promoting emotional balance.

Ingredients:

- 5 drops Lemongrass
- 5 drops Frankincense
- 5 drops Lavender
- 10 drops Jojoba oil (or another carrier oil)

Directions:

1. In a small glass roll-on bottle (about 10 ml), add the essential oils.
2. Fill the remainder of the bottle with jojoba oil.
3. Secure the cap and shake gently to mix.
4. Apply to pulse points (wrists, behind the ears, or on the back of the neck) whenever needed.

Benefits:

- Lemongrass: Energizing and cleansing properties that can help reduce fatigue and improve circulation.
- Frankincense: Calming and grounding, helpful for stress reduction and boosting mood.

- Lavender: Relaxing and balancing, promoting better sleep and stress relief.

2. Wintergreen and Sandalwood Relaxation Bath Soak

A warm bath with this blend can help ease the physical symptoms of hypothyroidism, such as joint pain and fatigue.

Ingredients:

- 4 drops Wintergreen
- 3 drops Sandalwood
- 1 tablespoon Epsom salt (for muscle relaxation)
- 1 tablespoon Coconut oil (for skin hydration)

Directions:

1. In a small bowl, mix the essential oils with the coconut oil and Epsom salt.
2. Add the mixture to a warm bath and stir to dissolve.
3. Soak for at least 20 minutes, allowing the oils to absorb into your skin.

Benefits:

- Wintergreen: Soothing and analgesic, helping to relieve muscle pain and tension.
- Sandalwood: Calming and grounding, promoting relaxation and helping to ease stress.

3. Stimulating Thyroid Massage Oil

This blend can be massaged into the neck area (where the thyroid is located) to promote circulation and support energy levels.

Ingredients:

- 3 drops Lemongrass
- 3 drops Frankincense
- 2 drops Lavender
- 15 ml Sweet almond oil (or your preferred carrier oil)

Instructions:

1. Mix all essential oils into the sweet almond oil.
2. Gently massage a few drops into the neck and chest area, where the thyroid is located.
3. Repeat daily or as needed.

Benefits:

- Lemongrass: Helps stimulate circulation and refresh the body.
- Frankincense: Grounding and soothing, beneficial for promoting a sense of calm and balance.
- Lavender: Known for its calming effects, helping to reduce stress and promote a sense of well-being.

4. Energizing Diffuser Blend

A diffuser blend can help create a calming environment that enhances energy and reduces mental fatigue.

Ingredients:

- 3 drops Lemongrass
- 2 drops Frankincense
- 2 drops Lavender
- 2 drops Sandalwood

Directions:

1. Add the essential oils to your diffuser with the appropriate amount of water.
2. Turn on the diffuser and let the blend fill the room.
3. Use as needed to create an uplifting and calming atmosphere.

Benefits:

- Lemongrass: Invigorating and energizing, stimulating mental clarity.
- Frankincense: Uplifting and calming, promoting mental clarity and grounding emotions.
- Lavender: Relaxing, which helps reduce stress and anxiety.
- Sandalwood: A grounding oil that promotes mental clarity and emotional balance.

5. Hypothyroid Relief Foot Soak

A relaxing foot soak to help alleviate the fatigue, stress, and muscle discomfort that often accompany hypothyroidism.

Ingredients:

- 4 drops Wintergreen
- 3 drops Lavender
- 2 drops Sandalwood
- 1/2 cup Epsom salt
- Warm water

Instructions:

1. In a foot basin, dissolve Epsom salt in warm water.
2. Add the essential oils and stir to combine.
3. Soak your feet for 15-20 minutes to enjoy a soothing and relaxing experience.

Benefits:

- Wintergreen: Reduces discomfort in joints and muscles.
- Lavender: Calms the mind and promotes relaxation.
- Sandalwood: Grounds and relaxes the body, reducing stress and fatigue.

Important Notes:

- Always do a patch test when using essential oils for the first time to ensure no allergic reaction occurs.

- Consult with a healthcare provider before using essential oils for therapeutic purposes, especially if you have a medical condition like hypothyroidism.
- These blends should be used as complementary support, not as a medical treatment replacement.

These recipes aim to create a balanced environment, promote relaxation, and address some symptoms commonly associated with hypothyroidism, such as fatigue and stress.

Several other essential oils can be used to support the hypothalamus and thyroid health, in addition to the ones mentioned. These oils can help balance hormones, support energy levels, improve mood, and reduce stress. Here are some essential oils that may be beneficial:

1. Clary Sage

- **Benefits**: Clary Sage is well-known for its hormone-balancing properties. It is often used to support the endocrine system, including the thyroid and adrenal glands. It may help reduce symptoms of hormonal imbalance like mood swings, fatigue, and anxiety.
- **How to Use**: Diffuse in the air, add a few drops to a carrier oil for massage, or apply to pulse points.

2. Basil

- **Benefits**: Basil oil is energizing and can help stimulate the thyroid, increase mental clarity, and reduce feelings of fatigue. It also has adaptogenic properties, which can help the body adapt to stress.

- **How to Use**: Diffuse or dilute with a carrier oil for topical application on areas like the back of the neck, which may help with thyroid health.

3. Geranium

- **Benefits**: Geranium essential oil is known for its hormone-regulating properties. It helps promote emotional balance and reduce stress, which is important for thyroid health, as chronic stress can worsen thyroid issues.
- **How to Use**: Diffuse or dilute with a carrier oil for massage on the chest or abdomen area.

4. Cypress

- **Benefits**: Cypress essential oil is supportive for the circulatory and lymphatic systems. It can promote detoxification and improve blood flow, which may help support thyroid function.
- **How to Use**: Use it in a diffuser or dilute it for topical application to the lymphatic system or along the thyroid area.

5. Myrrh

- **Benefits**: Myrrh oil has anti-inflammatory and antioxidant properties that can support the immune system, which may be helpful in thyroid conditions like Hashimoto's disease or autoimmune thyroid issues. It can also improve circulation.
- **How to Use**: Diffuse or dilute with a carrier oil and apply to pulse points or the thyroid area.

6. Thyme

- **Benefits**: Thyme essential oil has antimicrobial and stimulating properties. It can help stimulate the thyroid gland and support overall metabolic function. Thyme is also known to have adaptogenic qualities, which can assist in balancing hormone levels.
- **How to Use**: Dilute with a carrier oil and apply to the neck area or diffuse to stimulate the thyroid.

7. Rosemary

- **Benefits**: Rosemary is a powerful herb for stimulating circulation and supporting the thyroid. It can increase mental clarity, energy, and focus, which are often needed when dealing with hypothyroid symptoms.
- **How to Use**: Diffuse or massage diluted rosemary oil into the neck and upper chest area.

8. Peppermint

- **Benefits**: Peppermint oil is known for its invigorating and cooling properties. It can help relieve fatigue, reduce mental fog, and promote better circulation, which is important for thyroid function.
- **How to Use**: Diffuse, apply diluted oil to the temples, neck, or chest, or use in a bath to revitalize and refresh.

9. Jasmine

- **Benefits**: Jasmine essential oil helps with emotional balance and can alleviate anxiety and depression, which are common in thyroid disorders. It also has a calming effect on the nervous system.
- **How to Use**: Use in a diffuser or dilute with a carrier oil and apply to pulse points.

10. Bergamot

- **Benefits**: Bergamot is a citrus oil that helps balance the endocrine system, promote mental clarity, and reduce stress. It can be particularly helpful for those with hypothyroidism who experience mood swings or depression.
- **How to Use**: Diffuse or use topically (diluted) for mood enhancement.

How to Use These Essential Oils:

1. **Diffusion**: Add 3-5 drops of your chosen essential oil(s) to a diffuser. This method helps you inhale the oils, which can provide benefits for mood, mental clarity, and relaxation.
2. **Topical Application**: Always dilute essential oils with a carrier oil (such as coconut oil, jojoba oil, or sweet almond oil) before applying them to the skin. For thyroid support, you can apply the diluted oils around the neck area, where the thyroid is located, or to pulse points (wrists, temples, or behind the ears).

3. **Bath**: Add a few drops of essential oils to a warm bath (diluted in a carrier oil or Epsom salts) to promote relaxation and ease any tension.
4. **Massage**: Mix essential oils with a carrier oil and massage into areas of the body that may need support, such as the neck, shoulders, or lower back.

Important Considerations:

- **Patch Test**: Always do a patch test before applying essential oils to larger areas of skin to avoid any adverse reactions.
- **Consultation with a Healthcare Provider**: If you have hypothyroidism or any thyroid-related issues, it is important to consult with a healthcare provider before using essential oils as a complementary treatment.
- **Consistency**: Using essential oils consistently as part of a holistic approach to health can have positive effects, but they should not replace prescribed medical treatment.

These essential oils, when used thoughtfully, can support the thyroid and hypothalamus by helping with stress management, energy, hormone balance, and overall wellness.

Here are two simple and effective recipes using **Bergamot Essential Oil** for hypothyroidism and **Jasmine Essential Oil** for hyperthyroidism. These recipes address the symptoms and emotional imbalances often associated with each condition.

1. Hypothyroidism Support Recipe with Bergamot

Bergamot is known for its uplifting and mood-balancing properties, which can be particularly helpful for individuals with hypothyroidism who may experience fatigue, depression, or low energy levels.

Hypothyroidism Uplifting Roll-On Blend

This roll-on blend is great for promoting energy, reducing stress, and lifting mood when you need a quick pick-me-up throughout the day.

Ingredients:

- 6 drops **Bergamot** Essential Oil
- 4 drops **Lavender** Essential Oil (for relaxation and calming)
- 1 tablespoon **Jojoba oil** (or other carrier oil)

Instructions:

1. In a 10 ml roll-on bottle, add **Bergamot** and **Lavender** essential oils.
2. Fill the bottle with **Jojoba oil** or another carrier oil.
3. Secure the cap and gently shake to blend.
4. Apply to pulse points (wrists, behind the ears, or on the back of the neck) throughout the day when you need an energy boost and emotional support.

Benefits:

- **Bergamot**: Uplifting and stress-relieving, helps improve mood and reduce feelings of anxiety and fatigue.
- **Lavender**: Calms the nervous system, helping with stress and promoting relaxation.

2. Hyperthyroidism Support Recipe with Jasmine

Jasmine essential oil is soothing, making it an excellent choice for individuals with hyperthyroidism who may experience symptoms like anxiety, irritability, and nervous energy.

Hyperthyroidism Calming Bath Soak with Jasmine

This bath soak is perfect for calming the mind and body, reducing agitation, and promoting relaxation for individuals with hyperthyroidism.

Ingredients:

- 5 drops **Jasmine** Essential Oil
- 4 drops **Lavender** Essential Oil (for additional calming effects)
- 1 tablespoon **Epsom salt** (to help relax muscles and promote detoxification)
- 1 tablespoon **Coconut oil** (to help dilute the oils and moisturize the skin)

Instructions:

1. In a small bowl, mix the **Jasmine** and **Lavender** essential oils with the **Coconut oil**.
2. Add the **Epsom salt** and stir to combine.
3. Add the mixture to your warm bath water and stir to disperse the oils.
4. Soak in the bath for 20-30 minutes, focusing on deep breathing and allowing your body to relax.

Benefits:

- **Jasmine**: Soothes the nervous system, helping reduce anxiety, irritability, and emotional tension.
- **Lavender**: Provides a calming effect to help ease restlessness and promote better sleep.
- **Epsom salt**: Helps to relax muscles and detoxify the body, supporting overall well-being.

Important Notes:

- **Hypothyroidism (Bergamot)**: People with hypothyroidism may benefit from the mood-lifting and energizing properties of Bergamot, especially if fatigue and depression are present.
- **Hyperthyroidism (Jasmine)**: Jasmine helps reduce the anxiety, agitation, and nervous energy that are often experienced in hyperthyroidism.
- **Carrier Oils**: When using essential oils topically, always dilute them with a carrier oil such as **Jojoba**

oil, **Sweet almond oil**, or **Coconut oil** to avoid skin irritation.
- **Consult a Healthcare Provider**: Essential oils should be used as a complementary therapy, not as a medical treatment replacement. Always check with your healthcare provider if you have thyroid conditions.

These essential oil recipes can help support the emotional and physical well-being of individuals with hypothyroidism and hyperthyroidism, creating a more balanced and soothing environment.

Essential oils provide natural support for the hypothalamus and thyroid, helping restore balance and alleviate symptoms. However, they should not replace professional medical advice or treatment. Always perform a patch test before using any essential oil and consult a healthcare provider for personalized recommendations.

CHAPTER TWELVE

Essential Oils For Constipation And Flatulence

It is estimated that over 4 million people in the United States suffer from constipation, making it the most common digestive complaint. Over two million doctor visits annually are due to this uncomfortable condition. Constipation occurs when bowel movements are infrequent or the stool is hard and difficult to pass.

The hard, dry stool results from the colon malfunctioning, absorbing too much water. While it may seem contradictory to the common advice to "drink more water," this guidance remains accurate. The colon's muscle contractions may be too slow, causing the stool to move sluggishly through the digestive tract. As a result, excessive water is absorbed.

Causes of Constipation may stem from any of the following factors:

- Lack of suitable exercise
- Insufficient fluid intake
- Inadequate dietary fiber
- Intestinal dysfunction
- Laxative misuse
- Side effects of medications
- Irritable bowel syndrome (IBS)

Symptoms of Constipation

- Difficult or painful bowel movements

- Feeling bloated
- Fatigue or sluggishness
- Cramps

Treatment The appropriate treatment for constipation depends on one's overall health and may involve dietary changes, regular exercise, and/or medications.

Essential Oils for Constipation

Essential oils can affect individuals differently, so it's important to experiment and find what works best. Always perform a patch test before using essential oils to ensure you do not have an allergic reaction. If redness, itching, burning, or swelling occurs, immediately wash the area with mild soap and warm water. Consult your healthcare provider before incorporating essential oils into your routine.

Recommended Essential Oils for Constipation Relief

- **Ginger Essential Oil**: Known for its ability to settle an upset stomach, Ginger Essential Oil can also help relieve constipation. Mix 3 to 5 drops with 1 ounce of carrier oil, such as coconut or jojoba oil. Apply a few drops to your hand and gently massage the mixture onto your abdomen. Repeat 3 or more times daily as needed.
- **Helichrysum Essential Oil**: This oil may ease constipation when used topically. Mix 2 drops with 1 teaspoon of carrier oil (e.g., sweet almond oil). Warm the mixture slightly, then massage it onto your abdomen and lower stomach area. Use it after your morning shower and again before bed.

- **Fennel Essential Oil**: Fennel oil is effective for constipation relief. Combine 3 drops with 1 ounce of carrier oil, mix thoroughly, and massage onto the abdomen 2 to 3 times a day.
- **Peppermint Essential Oil**: Peppermint oil relaxes the muscles in the digestive tract, promoting bowel movements. Blend 2 to 3 drops with 1 tablespoon of warmed carrier oil (such as avocado or olive oil) and massage into the stomach and lower abdomen. Repeat 2 to 3 times daily until symptoms improve.

Other helpful essential oils include Rosemary Essential Oil and Lemon Essential Oil.

Flatulence

Flatulence, commonly known as passing gas or farting, is caused by a buildup of gas in the intestinal tract. While it can be a source of embarrassment, it is a normal bodily function. Several essential oils can be applied to the stomach and lower abdomen to help relieve gas buildup. These include Angelica Root, Cardamom, Caraway, Coriander, Fennel, Lavender, Lemongrass, Peppermint, and Spearmint. Below are recipes using three oils as examples; similar methods can be applied to others.

Essential Oils for Flatulence

Angelica Root Essential Oil Recipe

- Add 3 to 5 drops of Angelica Root Essential Oil to 1 tablespoon of warmed carrier oil. Mix well and apply to the lower abdomen. Gently rub in a downward circular motion. Use before bedtime and first thing in the morning (after your shower).

Cardamom Essential Oil Aids Digestion Recipe

- Used for over 4,000 years, Cardamom Essential Oil aids digestion. Mix 4 drops with 2 ounces of warmed Macadamia Oil or another carrier oil of your choice. Gently massage a small amount onto your lower abdomen.

Lemongrass Essential Oil Recipe to Relieve Stomach Gas

- Lemongrass Essential Oil supports healthy gastrointestinal function and can relieve gas, stomach discomfort, indigestion, and flatulence.
-
- Combine 3 to 4 drops with 1 ounce of warmed carrier oil. Mix thoroughly and gently massage the lower abdomen.

By incorporating these essential oils into your wellness routine, you may find relief from the discomfort of constipation and flatulence.

CHAPTER THIRTEEN

Diarrhea And Loose Bowels

Diarrhea is the frequent expulsion of watery stool, which is often accompanied by cramps, bloating, and an unease of needing to go. Diarrhea can be acute, lasting for several days, or it can be chronic, lasting several weeks.

Acute diarrhea is generally caused by infections or dietary indiscretions, whereas chronic diarrhea may involve digestive disorders or stress-related issues.

The common causes of diarrhea include the following:

Viral or bacterial infections

Food intolerances(lactose intolerance)

Medications (antibiotics)

Stress and anxiety

Digestive disorders (Irritable Bowel Syndrome, Crohn's disease)

Contaminated food or water

There are essential oils, when used appropriately, that can help soothe digestive upset, relieve cramping, and reduce associated inflammation. Here is a list of ten essential oils: Peppermint, Ginger, Chamomile, Lemon, Fennel,
 Coriander Seed, Tea Tree, Lavender, Basil, and Cardamom.

Peppermint Essential Oil is a powerful antispasmodic. It calms the muscles of the gastrointestinal tract and eases cramps and bloating.

What You Will Need:

One drop of high-quality Peppermint Essential Oil

One teaspoon of a carrier oil (Jojoba or Olive Oil)

Directions:

Mix these and gently massage clockwise over your abdomen. Do this twice a day. If you are experiencing a rough bout of pain, do it every hour until you feel relief. Generally, you would not have to do this more than 3 or 4 times. If you are still discomforted, talk to your medical doctor.

Ginger Essential Oil stimulates digestion, reduces nausea, and relieves inflammation in the stomach. Some aromatherapists recommend using a few drops of Ginger Essential Oil in a diffuser. Place the diffuser in a room. However, I feel it is not nearly as effective as direct application to the abdomen.

What You Will Need:

5 drops of Ginger Essential Oil

1 ounce of carrier oil (Sweet Almond Oil or Olive Oil

A small, dark brown bottle for mixing and storage.

Directions:

Place the Ginger Essential Oil in the bottle.

Add the carrier oil. Place the top on the bottle and shake to mix the oil.

Apply a small amount to the abdomen. Rub the area in a gentle circular motion.

Chamomile Essential Oil, known for its calming qualities, has been used for thousands of years. In addition to its calming qualities, it is known for its anti-inflammatory properties as well as an aid to the digestive system. Today, there are two primary species of Chamomile used for medicinal purposes: Roman Chamomile and German Chamomile. Even though they share similar properties, they are botanically distinct and differ in strength and uses. We will talk about Roman Chamomile and its use for abdominal pain relief, stress-induced diarrhea, upset stomach, and colic.

Roman Chamomile has an apple-like fragrance, and because it is mild and gentle, it is preferred for children and sensitive individuals.

Children's Blend for Upset Stomach

The following blend is recommended for children four years old and up. Remember to do a patch test and consult your medical doctor.

What You Will Need

2 drops of Roman Chamomile Essential Oil
1 drop of Lavender Essential Oil
1 drop of Cardamom Essential Oil
1 ounce of a carrier oil

Directions:

Mix the oils and carrier oil.
Apply a small amount to the abdomen and feet. Gently massage the oils into the skin. If any irritation occurs,

discontinue use. It may be applied to adults as well as children.

Lemon Essential Oil is an excellent mild detoxifier. It supports lymphatic drainage and restores energy after a digestive upset. It may be used for direct inhalation and as a topical application.

What You Will Need

A diffuser

5 to 8 drops of Lemon Essential Oil
Add the oil to the diffuser. Follow the directions for using the diffuser.
Use during a digestive upset or right after.

If you do not have a diffuser, place 4 to 5 drops of the Leomon Essential Oil on a small cloth for direct inhalation. Slowly breathe in and out for 3 to 5 minutes. Select your comfort level.

Fennel Essential Oil's highly aromatic flavor makes it a popular gut remedy. Besides its culinary uses, Fennel has traditionally been used to combat digestive issues such as gas and bloating. Here is a recipe for a Fennel Digestive Support Blend.

What You Will Need

2 drops of Fennel Essential Oil

2 drops of Peppermint Essential Oil

2 drops of Ginger Essential Oil

1 tablespoon of fractionated coconut oil

Directions:

Combine all the oils in a dark glass roller bottle. Shake to blend. Apply a gentle clockwise massage to your abdomen after meals. Do this after each meal.

Note: Avoid using Fennel if pregnant and with children under the age of 6.

Fennel For Nervous Diarrhea

Use this recipe before or after each meal.

What You Will Need

4 drops of Roman Chamomile Essential Oil
3 drops of Lavender Essential Oil
2 drops of Coriander Seed Essential Oil
3 drops of Cardamom Essential Oil
1 ounce of carrier oil

Directions

Mix all the ingredients. Gently rub two or three drops on the abdomen.

Coriander Seed Essential Oil As a Digestive Soother

Coriander is antispasmodic, aids in one's digestion, and helps stop flatulence.

What You Will Need

4 drops of Coriander Seed Essential Oil

1 teaspoon of carrier oil (Sweet Almond Oil blends nicely with Coriander).

Cardamom Essential Oil For Warming the Belly-A Rub

What You Will Need

5 drops of Cardamom Essential Oil
3 drops of Sweet Orange Essential Oil
1 ½ teaspoons of Jojoba or Olive Oil

Directions

In a small dish or dark brown bottle, combine the ingredients. Shake or stir to mix.

Add a couple of drops to your hands and rub them together to warm the oils.

Gently rub onto your stomach. Do this after a meal or when you are experiencing digestive upset.

Tea Tree Essential Oil For Calming Massage

This recipe is designed to calm and soothe the nerves, thus improving the digestive processes.

What You Will Need

5 drops of Tea Tree Essential Oil
3 drops of Roman Chamomile Essential Oil
1 ½ teaspoons of Fractionated Coconut Oil

Directions

Thoroughly mix the oils and carrier oil.

Place a couple of drops on the lower back and gently massage. Then, place a couple of drops on the abdomen and massage.

Lavender Gentle Gut Calmer

What You Will Need

5 drops Lavender essential oil
1 tablespoon grapeseed oil

Directions

Mix the ingredients and gently massage them onto the abdomen and lower back just before going to bed and during digestive distress.

Basil Relief Blend for Intestinal Cramps

What You Will Need

3 drops of Basil Essential Oil
2 drops of Ginger Essential Oil
1 tablespoon of Sesame Oil or Almond Oil

Directions

Mix the ingredients. Warm them and then apply to the abdomen in slow circular motions. Apply 1 to 2 times during acute digestive issues.

CHAPTER FIFTEEN

Embarrassing Rosacea

Due to their anti-inflammatory and antibacterial qualities, essential oils may help manage the occurrence of Rosacea. It is estimated that 14 million adults in the United States are affected by Rosacea. So, what is Rosacea?

Rosacea is an inflammatory skin condition. Its symptoms include the following:

- Redness on the face
- Sudden flushing
- Sudden blushing
- Pimples
- Thick skin on the nose
- Visible blood vessels

Several things may set it off. Among the triggers are the following:

- Sun
- Heat
- Spicy foods
- Stress
- Skincare products that are alcohol-based
- Blood pressure medications
- Steroids applied directly to the skin

The following eleven recipes are designed to be calming, anti-inflammatory, and skin-barrier supportive. They are diluted for facial use.

You will need a small brown glass bottle with a stopper and an eyedropper,

Four carrier oils are suggested. In the following recipes, you are to choose one carrier oil to use. You may use a different carrier oil each time.

The Carrier Oils

Jojoba Oil – Good for skin balancing and is non-comedogenic
Rosehip Seed Oil – Supports skin repair
Calendula Infused Oil – Soothing
Sweet Almond Oil – Hydrates the skin
Tamanu – Pain relief

Frankincense, tea tree, chamomile, lavender, helichrysum, rose otto, sandalwood, citrus, neroli, carrot seed, and manuka are recommended essential oils to help reduce the embarrassing redness and swelling associated with Rosacea.

Recipes for Rosacea Relief

Recipe Number One

<u>What You Will Need</u>

1 clean, sterilized 2-ounce dark glass bottle with a stopper
45 drops of German Chamomile Essential Oil
35 drops of Manuka Essential Oil

Optional: 2-3 drops of Rose or Lavender Essential Oil (for a sweeter scent)

Directions:

Add the German Chamomile and Manuka essential oils to the sterilized bottle.

Replace the stopper and shake the bottle until the oils are well mixed.

Add 12 to 15 drops of the blended oils to a carrier oil of your choice, such as Jojoba or Tamanu oil.

Add 2-3 drops of Rose or Lavender Essential Oil for fragrance if desired.

Apply one or two drops of the mixture to clean skin in the morning or at bedtime.

Recipe Number Two

What You Will Need:

2 drops of Lavender Essential Oil
1 drop of German Chamomile Essential Oil
1 drop of Helichrysum Essential Oil
1 tablespoon of a carrier oil
1 small glass brown bottle for mixing,

Directions
Combine all the ingredients in the glass bottle. Insert the top, and shake well.

For Rosacea relief, apply 1 to 2 drops to the impacted area. Do this twice daily,

Recipe Number Three

What You Will Need:

2 drops of Roman Chamomile Essential Oil
1 drop of Rose Otto Essential Oil
1 drop of Frankincense
1 tablespoon of carrier oil
1 small brown glass bottle with a stopper

Directions
Combine all the ingredients in the bottle, replace the stopper, and shake the bottle until the ingredients are thoroughly mixed.
To lessen redness, add one drop to the infected area and gently massage it into the skin.

Recipe Number Four

What You Will Need:
2 drops of Helichrysum Essential Oil
1 drop of Lavender Essential Oil
1 drop of Sandalwood Essential Oil
1 Tablespoon of carrier oil

Directions

Mix the essential oils with carrier oil.
Apply 1 to 2 drops to the area and gently massage to help skin barrier repair.

Recipe Number Five

What You Will Need

1 drop of German Chamomile Essential Oil
1 drop of Citrus Essential Oil
2 drops of Lavender Essential Oil
1 Tablespoon of carrier oil

Directions

Mix all the ingredients. To calm the inflammation, add 1 drop to the area and gently rub it in.

Recipe Number Six

What You Will Need

1 drop of Rose Otto Essential Oil
1 drop of Helichrysum Essential Oil
2 drops of Frankincense Essential Oil
1 Tablespoon of carrier oil

Directions

Thoroughly mix the oils. Apply a small amount to your skin at bedtime.

Recipe Number Seven

<u>What You Will Need</u>

1 Tablespoon of pure aloe vera gel
2 drops of Lavender Essential Oil
1 drop of German Chamomile Essential Oil
1 drop of Tea Tree Essential Oil (Use this only if there is no sensitivity)

Directions

Mix all the oils. Store in refrigerator for at least one hour. Then apply a thin layer to your Rosacea.

Recipe Number Eight

<u>What You Will Need</u>

1 drop of Neroli Essential Oil
1 drop of Rose Otto Essential Oil
2 drops of Roman Chamomile Essential Oil
1 Tablespoon of carrier oil

Directions

Mix and add 1 drop to the enflamed area.

Recipe Number Nine

<u>What You Will Need</u>

1 drop of Carrot Seed Essential Oil
1 drop of Lavender Essential Oil
1 drop of Frankincense Essential Oil
1 Tablespoon of carrier oil

Directions

Mix all the ingredients. Once oils are well mixed, apply them to the skin to help tone it.

Recipe Ten

<u>What You Will Need</u>

2 drops of Lavender Essential Oil
1 drop of Sandalwood
1 drop of Roman Essential Oil
1 Tablespoon of Infused Calendula Oil

Directions

Mix thoroughly. Carefully apply a thin layer to the infected skin.

Additional Tips To Help Manage Rosacea

- **Sun Protection:** Always use a broad-spectrum sunscreen to minimize exposure to one of the primary triggers.
- **Stress Management:** Engage in relaxation techniques such as yoga or meditation to reduce stress.

- **Dietary Awareness:** Avoid spicy foods and monitor your diet to identify and eliminate potential food triggers.
- **Gentle Skincare:** opt for mild, alcohol-free skincare products to avoid further irritation.
- **Combining essential** oils with careful lifestyle adjustments, you may find relief from Rosacea and improve your overall skin health.
- **Remember to always** check with your medical doctor if you have issues or questions.

CHAPTER SIXTEEN

Etcetera & Etcetera

As with many other things, there is always something more to say. The subject of essential oils is certainly among those. What follows is a short collection of all things essential oils.

Essential Oil Remedy for Insect Bites

Combine the following oils in a dark-colored glass bottle with a stopper. Be sure the bottle has been sterilized.

- 6 drops of Lavender Essential Oil
- 8 drops of Cedarwood Essential Oil
- 8 drops of Patchouli Essential Oil
- 10 drops of Tea Tree Essential Oil
- 6 drops of Geranium Essential Oil
- 20 drops of Eucalyptus Essential Oil
- 3 ounces of carrier oil

Thoroughly mix the ingredients before each use. A technique my aromatherapist and teacher taught me was to hold the bottle of oil in my hand for a couple of minutes before applying. This is a gentle warming of the oils.

The Wonderful Turmeric Essential Oil

Archaeological evidence dates the use of Turmeric for medicinal and ceremonial purposes at least 4,000 years ago. Turmeric is said to support the immune system. It is used to improve the overall quality of the skin and hair. It helps support the body's recovery processes from injuries and illnesses.

Add 2 to 3 drops of Turmeric Essential Oil to a diffuser to help lessen coughing associated with colds.

For those with respiratory issues, Turmeric may offer some real relief. Mix 10 drops of Turmeric Essential Oil with the following essential oils:

6 drops of Ginger Essential Oil
6 drops of Eucalyptus Essential Oil
4 drops of Clary Sage Essential Oil

Mix these in a dark-colored glass bottle.

To use on your chest, add 4 ounces of Jojoba carrier oil and thoroughly mix. Perform a patch test on your wrist. If no problems arise, take a couple of drops and gently rub them onto your chest. Do this a couple of times a day, especially before bed.

To use in a diffuser, add 2 to 3 drops (omit the Jojoba Oil). Sit in a room with the diffuser running and slowly inhale to bring breathing relief.

Moringa Essential Oil

Moringa, an important food source, is native to India. Its high nutritional value makes it a very desirable plant. Its antioxidant qualities help protect cells from damage. It appears to have a positive effect on asthma, diabetes, cholesterol levels, constipation, and headaches. Because of its long list of benefits, it is sometimes called "The Miracle Tree."

Hair Care Recipe

Moringa is especially helpful for skin and hair. Here is a recipe for fixing hair issues:

Ingredients:

2 cups of a carrier oil with excellent moisturizing qualities

10 to 15 drops of Moringa Essential Oil

5 to 10 drops of Lavender Essential Oil

Directions:

1. Mix the oils in a glass bowl or bottle.
2. Apply to clean hair and gently massage it into the roots.
3. Cover hair with a shower cap and leave on overnight.
4. Shampoo and condition hair as usual.
5. Optionally, heat this mixture for a few seconds in a microwave before applying. Some people enjoy the heightened scent that heating gives the oils.

Essential Oils and Inguinal Hernia

An inguinal hernia affects approximately 27% of men and 3% of women. There are around 899,000 inguinal hernia surgeries annually. Depending on the situation, surgery may not always be necessary. Specific exercises suggested by a physical therapist and approved by a medical doctor may help. The application of certain essential oils may reduce the need for surgery. As always, consult your medical doctor first.

Inguinal Hernia Relief Recipe

Ingredients:

- 10 drops of Cypress Essential Oil
- 10 drops of Lavender Essential Oil
- 8 drops of Frankincense Essential Oil
- 6 drops of Geranium Essential Oil
- 1 to 2 ounces of a carrier oil of your choice

Directions:

1. Mix these oils in a dark glass bottle. If you don't have a bottle, use a sterilized dish.
2. If using a bottle, ensure the cap is tight and shake the bottle for a full minute. If using a dish, sanitize the stirrer and mix thoroughly.
3. Slightly warm the mixed oils by holding the bottle in your hands for a couple of minutes or pre-warming the dish before adding the oils.
4. Gently massage a couple of drops into the hernia area. Do this nightly.

AUTHOR'S NOTE

I gratefully acknowledge the team behind ChatGPT, developed by OpenAI, for its invaluable assistance with spelling, sentence structure, and tone. Their support has saved me countless hours of work.

N.W.W., Ph.D.

www.ingramcontent.com/pod-product-compliance
Lightning Source LLC
Chambersburg PA
CBHW061654040426
42446CB00010B/1728